RELIGIOUS BELIEF

... solution via
and logical an
of infinity. I
theory—one th
creation and e.
hand and evolu , MEYER
about what constitutes ... sin.

The question of waning belief in angels and evils is boldly associated with the scientific search for intelligent extraterrestrial life. Eschatology is correlated with scientific postulates concerning the existence of other dimensional systems. A new theory about the resurrection of Jesus is offered. And finally, the vexing problem of the double consciousness of Jesus—one human, one divine—is examined in the light of Einstein's general theory of relativity.

This breakthrough book is aimed at all Christians who hold traditional religious beliefs that they may live more comfortably in the modern scientific world.

CHARLES R. MEYER, a priest of the Archdiocese of Chicago, received a masters degree in philosophy and a doctorate in theology from St. Mary of the Lake Seminary, Mundelein, Ill. He pursued post-doctoral studies at the Gregorian University in Rome. Presently professor of systematic theology at St. Mary of the Lake he is the author of a number of books including *A Contemporary Theology of Grace*, *The Touch of God: A Theological Analysis of Religious Experience* and *What a Modern Catholic Believes about the Holy Spirit*.

Religious
Belief
in a
Scientific
Age

by
Charles R. Meyer

THE THOMAS MORE PRESS
Chicago, Illinois

ISBN 0-88347-152-3

CONTENTS

79253

Chapter I

THE ACCULTURATION OF BELIEF

THE history of religious speculation reveals the fact that theology can best be defined as the acculturation of belief. This means that the believer must be a person who is fully and in every way situated in his or her own world. Just because a person is a believer does not mean that he or she can abdicate his or her own racial, ethnic or cultural heritage. This imperative has always more or less been taken for granted in the history of theology. But today, in an era of heightened racial and ethnic awareness, it becomes especially important in any theological enterprise.

We have only to indulge in minimal self-examination to see that our consciousness is thoroughly impregnated by the values and philosophy of the era and culture in which we are situated. We are creatures of place and time. And often our faith, our religious belief, is stored in a separate psychic compartment so as not to be tarnished by the world in which we live.

It is always necessary to carefully distinguish between faith and theology. Faith is the ground of theology: it is what theology is all about. But faith is not explainable except in terms of some kind of theology. Theology is the knowledge inherent in faith lifted into the clarity of conscious knowing.

7

As such, it cannot help but be tempered by both the age and locale in which it is expressed.

Everyone knows that while the substance and content of belief, when it is viewed as an adherence to a basic position or cause, might well be considered as absolute and unchanging, any formulation of what it implies for the individual has to be conditional and partial; it cannot exhaust completely the potential of the subjective condition, but in any given situation can answer only those questions which are perceived to be significant. Often in this connection one also encounters a hermeneutic circle: answers are conditioned by the questions that are asked; these in turn give rise to new questions, the answers to which may already be conditioned and determined by the initial responses, and so on. Experience teaches that every formulation eventually has to undergo ecdysis. Outmoded doctrinal formulations, acculturated to bygone ages and ill-suited to the modern scene, have to be shucked off, just as some reptiles shed their old skin or birds molt.

Every historian knows that interpretation and expression always have to be related not merely to the material that is being handled, but to the audience that is being addressed. It is clearly unfair to judge past events by current standards or values. The past must always be judged by its own standards. But the past as past is never fully retrievable. Our understanding of the past as affecting the present is what is significant, and in the pursuit of our historical task we often cannot help, though we ought not, interjecting some of our present opinions when dealing with the past. So the ideal is not often achieved, even when an honest effort is expended.

Let us turn to a case in point. We might expect to find in the writings of Paul, which are among the earliest in the New Testament, and closest to the time of Jesus himself, some detail about the life of Jesus and some of his sayings — perhaps some that we would not find in later sources because memory lapsed. But Paul's mission was to a Gentile culture and the historical Jesus belongs to Judaism. So it was not to Paul's purpose to tell us about Jesus' own mission to the Jews. Here we see the process of acculturation begun very early in the history of Christianity. We have another poignant example in the Gospel of John which was written against those who resented the translation of the original Christian ideas from the Hebrew to a Greek context. Many key dogmas have developed in the matrix of a definite culture or philosphy. Notable are the Trinitarian doctrine which (to put it, admittedly, in an oversimplified way) developed in the gnostic world of the Middle East and North Africa, and also the idea of the Incarnation which found a comfortable situs in the Neoplatonist dualism of the Greek empire. Every theologian knows how the formula of St. Cyril of Alexandria with reference to the one nature of the incarnate God eventually became heretical when the understanding of it was not modified after the Council of Chalcedon.

In our own day older formulations which originated in the ambit of a medieval mentality are being challenged by the modern spirit. Questions asked by past ages are quite different from today's concerns. The philosophical absolutism of the past is quite foreign to today's mentality. Conversely, the world today is comfortable with the tentative and the uncertain. It recognizes the possibility that everything in life may not be fully meaningful. There are segments of our society that even cultivate the meaningfulness of meaninglessness. People today value the personal and relational. Many are highly suspicious of organizations — particularly those clouded in a veil of secrecy, that impose dogmas that are inflexible and indulge in rituals that are not fully understood or appreciated. Today's society does not lust after what is final and definitive; it is rather content with what is transient and fleeting. People in our time prize autonomy and freedom highly. They are reluctant to give up their liberty in support of even the most worthwhile causes. The world today looks upon time as ruthlessly rectilinear, carefully avoiding the cyclic conceptualizations of the past. The young, especially, have left their imprint on our culture. Their preoccupation with the present seems at times almost obsessive. They thirst insatiably for new experiences. They do not seek new ideas or philosophies, but search for new ways of self-expression and unbridled sentience. They largely eschew the burden of commitment. Some even regard freedom as too heavy a price to pay for coping with the demands that it often imposes. But if there is anything that the modern world believes in, it is the theories and data put forth by current scientific investigation.

No one doubts that our culture is dominated today by science and technology. Science is now taught even at the lower levels of grade school. The most promising job opportunities lie in technological areas, or at least presuppose some technical know-how. If we can judge the world of the future by present trends, we can be sure that it will be one whose consciousness is immersed in scientific and technological concerns.

Just as the theologies of the past have developed in the matrices of successive philosophical systems, ranging from Platonism to existentialism, so the theology of the future will have to be developed in the context of scientific knowledge. The first philosophy that offered Christianity a bed to lie in was Platonism. Eventually it gave way to Aristotelianism. There have hardly ever been two other philosophies so opposed. For Platonism the idea is the only reality; the world exists as a reflection of the ideal. In Aristotelianism the world we experience is real and ideas, to be true, must conform to it. Aristotelianism became very influential in determining the future of Roman Catholic theology in the form known as Scholasticism which developed from a reflection upon the doctrine of the Stagirite by St. Thomas Aquinas and other theologians in late medieval and renaissance times. Other reactions to Aristotelian philosophy, such as Nominalism espoused by William of Ockham, Rocelin of Compiègne and Peter Abelard, and

Kantianism, which strongly influenced Fichte, Schelling and Hegel, had a definite impact on the development of Protestant theological methodology. Scholasticism still remains a shibboleth in Catholic theology. Attempts to restore it characterize official Church pronouncements and the writings of those who seek to reinstate metaphysical speculation, while attempts to replace it with a more humanistic outlook are evidenced in the works of theologians taken with existentialism.

Neither of these tendencies has been completely successful. Consequently, theological philosophy is experiencing chaos. Both neo-Scholasticism and existentialism tend to create an intellectual elite, cut off from the rest of the world, reveling in its own cant and thinking processes and seeking to influence society with its own value system. But this attempt has failed. Neither neo-Scholasticism nor existentialism can find a home that is comfortable in the Church of today, beset as it is with the post-Vatican II blues and blahs. These philosophies are too recondite for the average Christian to understand. He or she often prefer simply to return to the simple catechism formulas of yesteryear.

But people are initiated into science through the newspapers and other media. Schools make science courses mandatory from the early grades through several years at the secondary level. Scientific discoveries generally go unchallenged by the populace at large. If people are prone to accept anthing they hear today, I would suspect it would be the scientific data they receive through the media. It would seem then that the field of science might well be able to afford a viable and productive interface with theology.

Some precedent for this has already been set in the celebrated efforts of Pierre Teilhard de Chardin. Although his study was largely limited to the field of biology and evolution and how it might be connected with theology, nonetheless, his pioneering investigations have provided a viable model for future attempts at correlation. His genius really consists in wedding Marxist material- ism with Pauline Christology. Important for Chardin were the principles of dialectical material- ism; he viewed them as basic to the mechanism of evolution: opposites attract; quantative variations lead eventually to qualitative ones; every negation will eventually itself be negated. These form the fabric of Teilhard's notion of complexification, the idea that the disparate, simpler, smaller elements of the universe gradually gravitate toward a center and form larger, more complex, organized bodies. Tangential energy, or that which exhibits a more centrifugal vector, is slowly, through entropization, becoming radial or centripetal energy. The whole universe and its component parts are being drawn by an irresistible force toward a center. And that force is love, and that center is Christ. The ultimate name of the universe's game is Christogenesis, or the coming into being of the whole Christ, the mystic Christ, Christ the head uniting all creation to himself, Christ who has become all in all — that doctrine so dear to the heart of Paul.

Unfortunately, the adversative position taken in the past by scientists and theologians still stands as a challenge to anyone who would attempt to forge some kind of union. This position has been abetted by those in authority in the Church, and filtering down to ordinary believers, has found a certain resonance with them. In fact, in the past, many God-fearing people felt definitely threatened by the inroads of science and technology. In some quarters, technological developments have been viewed as the work of the devil who tempts mankind to be so proud as to think it can improve on the work of God in creation. Such a view was reflected in an incident that occurred during the reign of King Philip II of Spain. A suggestion was submitted to the royal court to make the rivers Tajo and Manzanares navigable. If ships could move all the way down these rivers, carrying produce from certain isolated areas inland, and on their return trip bring manufactured goods to this segment of the population, not only would the quality of life in these isolated lands be improved tremendously, but the economy of the whole country would be enhanced. But the ecclesiastical advisers of the king provoked a negative decision on the part of the commission that was set up to investigate the possibility of dredging the rivers. The ultimate reason given was that if God had so willed that these rivers should be navigable, he would have created them thus.

The antagonism that flourished between developing science and religion in the 19th century is well known. The Church in most of its denominational forms heartily resisted the growth of evolutionary theory. Creationism vs. evolution is an issue that is still agitated. Recent court battles give ample evidence that theories much less radical than Teilhard's would be rejected as blasphemous in certain quarters today.

Yet, in spite of this thinking, people do pose the question: "How can I live in the modern world, accept what it offers, and still consistently hold onto my religious convictions? Can I still believe that there is a heaven above and a hell below? Can I still accept the doctrine about angels and devils? Are my religious experiences genuine, or just aberrations of my subconscious? Is there really a God who is kind and gracious, or are my ideas about him just a projection of my wishes and desires in reaction to the ruthless concatenation of natural phenomena that encroach upon my life, my health and my mental stability? Can I really believe that Jesus is God when he seems to be so human? Can I believe that he is present in the eucharist when all I see and feel and taste are bread and wine? If the realities with which religion deals lie beyond the scope of any kind of empirical investigation, how can I put my faith and trust in them?"

I suppose that these people do realize that as we begin to attempt to correlate religious and scientific truth and methodology we are hampered by the heritage we have received from the past in both areas. Their outlook on truth itself is sufficiently diverse. Religion in general tends to regard truth as absolute, as unchanging and eternal. With respect to essentials there can be no openness to further development. The book is closed. If peripheral acculturation is permitted, it is largely in language, expression and ritual. Dogmas must remain intact; only the way they are expressed and celebrated can be modified.

Scientific truth, on the other hand, always has to be relative. Data are established and theories advanced only provisionally and contingently. Every scientist as such must maintain an openness to the possible future negation or at least modification of his discoveries and explanations. The scientist can never have the absolute and final word. Scientific dialogue must continue indefinitely. The investigator must remain undaunted by continual setbacks, rejection and total failure. Like nature itself he must carry on impassively, groping with indifference, now concentrating, now diversifying his efforts.

No one would be so naive as to think that both religion and science have remained true to their diverse speculative outlooks — that there has been no cross-fertilization, that religion has remained untouched by time and science is as fluid as time.

As a matter of fact, in its origins the Christian attitude seems to have been just the opposite of what we witness today. Now it subsists in a fabric of rigid dogmatism; but originally it seems to have entertained as one of its basic principles radical openness to God, a readiness to go along with

whatever happened, a steadfast refusal to stereo-
type God.

Indeed the Christian philosophy drastically
modified Jewish religious ideas and practices. This
happened despite Jesus' protest that he came to ful-
fill and not to destroy. That fulfillment did,
however, imply rejection of the ways that traditional Judaism had been adapted by the learned
Jewish contemporaries of Jesus, especially the Sad-
ducees and Pharisees. To them Jesus proposed what
must have seemed like a totally new outlook on
God and his dealings with the chosen people — and
indeed with the whole human race. One of the focal
points of Jesus' mission seems to have been to inculcate the notion that one must keep an open mind
in regard to the pronouncements of God. One of
the problems that Jesus experienced in fulfilling
this mission — a problem created especially by the
Pharisee party — was that a religious establishment
could possess and hand on the sum total of all
religious truth. Everyone could get along just fine if
nothing were added, nothing modified. One could,
as it were, get a handle on God by believing in the
promises and keeping the law — interpreted, of
course, by the Pharisees. Jesus excoriated this idea.
He called people's attention to the fact that so
often God is to be found where one would least expect him — in the company of sinners, with the
downtrodden and despicable, in the sullied and
tawdry events of human life. I believe that Barth is
right when he indicates that one of the key elements

in the preaching and mission of Jesus was to inculcate the truth that God is not what man would
be if man were God. If we couple this with
Rahner's idea that man is what God chose to be
when he decided not to appear in this world as
God, we have a pretty good idea of the flexibility
that the one who is called the founder of the
Christian religion — at least the one for whom it is
named — seemed to have not only permitted, but
encouraged.

But it is not only Christianity that has gravitated
toward the absolute and the rigid. Many of the
world's great religions, at least those that are based
on documents of one kind or another, have exhib-
ited this tendency. Look at conservative Judaism,
at Islam, at Hinduism. The dogmatism that modern Christianity evidences does not single it out as
unique among the great religions of the world. This
drift toward a closed mind, was, of course, not the
only violation of the seeming intent of the Master
that was to characterize the later development of
Christianity. One would wonder if Jesus returned
to earth today the way he visited it two millenia ago
if he would recognize at all the religion that bears
his name.

There seems, however, to have been one area
where Jesus himself was inflexible. If he highlighted an openness to the call of God, an invitation
to find and respect God everywhere, he did seem to
have himself a closed mind about faith. Once one
discovers the word of God, he must relentlessly adhere to it. Faith can never waver. What is believed

may be modified, but the act of belief may never falter. The true believer must accept and adhere firmly to the word of God wherever and however he perceives it.

The primitive Church caught some of this spirit of open-mindedness. For instance, its leaders decided not to impose Jewish legal obligations on Gentile converts. In the so-called Council of Jerusalem acculturation won a great victory. Paul, of course, was instrumental in successfully promoting this cause. But there was another side to Paul too. He seems to have become a kind of personal rule of faith for his people. We remember how he told some of them to be imitators of him as he was of Christ (and this was not a bad idea if he really knew Christ well enough to imitate him also in his open-mindedness) but he also taught that his own doctrine was the absolute and final word. Even if an angel from heaven were to descend and announce a doctrine different from his, that angel ought not to be believed, messenger from God though he might be [Gal. 1/8].

So there is some evidence that the trend toward absolutizing doctrinal positions, a trend that could rarely be correlated with acculturation, was already catching on in the early Church. Down through the centuries it waxed and waned. It posed a difficulty for the Reformers. But even in Protestantism one encounters wide variations, sometimes experiencing the excess of acculturation that has produced national churches, at other times the rigidity that takes the words of the Bible literally. But the defen-

sive position of the Roman church, sparked initially by the Reformation and fostered by political
challenges to the authority of the papacy, put it
more and more on the conservative and absolutist
side. We can see what it all led to when we consider
what happened to Matteo Ricci in China when he
tried to acculturate Catholicism in the 17th century
and was fantastically successful, or Roberto de'
Nobili when he tried the same thing among the
Brahmans in India — *Romanitá* triumphed. The
Latin mentality and mores were imposed upon
these peoples with a dreadful loss. Missionaries to
China were required to take an oath that they
would not indulge in the practice of "Chinese
rites," and so what might have been the largest
Christian nation in the world was cut off from the
Church. It was only in 1939 after the Roman
Church accepted the declaration of the Chinese
government that the respect paid to Kung and one's
ancestors constituted only a civil and cultural act,
and not a religious one, that missionaries began to
work freely again. But by then it was far too late.

In the Roman Church, through the 19th and
early 20th century, dogmatic absolutism became a
way of life. But after the Second Vatican Council
the Church experienced a greater pluralism in theological development. Theoretically the Church had
always maintained a position that there could be a
development and adaptation of dogma, but practically it has resisted such a phenomenon. After Vatican II, despite efforts of the magisterium jealously
to safeguard certain positions, highly respected

theologians like Karl Rahner have introduced the notion of a hierarchy of dogmatic truths, that is, that some truths ought to be considered more vital and relevant to the faith than others, that some are more appropriate for the times than others. Yet the trials of those who have attempted to put such an outlook into practice, theologians like Hans Küng and Edward Schillebeeckx, have led many to wonder if the magisterium has even to this day assimilated its own teaching about the development and adaptation of dogmatic truth.

But it is a fact that there is indeed a wide range of pluralism among the faithful in our time. There are some who live and believe as if Vatican II had never happened. Many, as sociological polls have revealed, manifest a minimum of adherence to the official Church's pronouncements on birth control (a point which is being made a kind of shibboleth of loyalty by current Church administration). Positions on the importance of the papacy in the governance of the Church, on the infallibility of the pope, in the authority of the diocesan bishop, on the freedom of the clergy, especially to marry, on the relationship of the local church to the national and universal Church vary widely, and reflect very diverse thinking on these matters in various regions of the world. In the United States, especially, is this divergence of opinion much in evidence. And history has shown that when a wide range of belief adherence exists in various segments of the Church, either the Church is split by schism, as happened in the case of East versus West in 1054, or by a de-

nominational splintering, such as occurred in the
Reformation, or the Church resolves these difficulties by accepting the status of pluralism, as happened, for instance, in the famous disputation *de
auxiliis* wherein the problem of how God retains
absolute mastery over the economy of salvation on
the one hand, and how the human will remains
totally free even under the influence of grace on the
other, was held for a number of decades in the presence of the pope himself. Ultimately it was decided
that all the divergent views could be considered
doctrinally acceptable, and the only outcome was a
decree forbidding any of the principals to brand the
others as heretical; or, finally, the Church resolves
the difficulty of doctrinal pluralism by an official
pronouncement outlawing one position or the other
or attempting a dogmatic synthesis of the issues
involved.

At any rate, it seems that a divergence of opinion
among the faithful is ultimately never ignored, nor
can it be. But until it is resolved doctrinal pluralism
can be a source of vexation to many. A fresh look
at the issues involved through the eyes of a neutral,
outside discipline like psychology or science is often
helpful. It can provide a basis for assuring essential
unity in the midst of a pluralism which is helpful to
growth.

When we try, with the help of an outside discipline, to see how theology will look in the future,
we are exercising our prophetic mission as Christians. It is my opinion that, sometime in the future,
diverse theological speculations of the present will

achieve that desired, essentially unified understanding and coherence under the aegis of science. Science will provide a matrix for future theological growth as philosophy did in the past.

During the time we are engaged with this book, let us be bold enough even to lay aside our Christian heritage, if we believe that it in any way involves prejudice — the prior judgment that Christian doctrine is not capable of complete acculturation, especially in a world that is dominated by a scientific outlook. Let us seek the openness of Jesus. Let us for a time stifle our natural appetite for the absolute, the final and complete and the comfortable. Let us try to be patient with the tentative, the provisional, the uncertain, the disturbing. For that may well be what this book will explore.

But if we really believe what Jesus was about, if we really accept the message that seemed to pervade his encounters with the Pharisees, his parables of reversal and his ignominious death, we will believe that even in this study we might be able to find out something more about God and his world. For is he not most often found, as Jesus teaches, where we least expect him to be?

Chapter II

SYMBOLS AND MYTHS

HOPE for a successful interface between theology and science, I believe, lies chiefly in the fact that both enterprises make an extensive use of symbols and myths. Though it may seem at first blush that science deals only with empirically verifiable truths just a little reflection will reveal that this is really not so. We know that often mathematics is involved in the argumentation and development of all the exact sciences. Physics and quantum mechanics could not exist without the calculus. Yet the language of mathematics is symbolism. Philosophers of science readily admit that what emerges from our laboratory experiments are not absolute laws dealing with hard and unchangeable and final facts, but rather estimations dealing with the behavioral patterns of matter. And these patterns seem best able to be explicitated and interpreted in terms of statistical analysis. When an experiment is performed, admittedly, not all the atoms or molecules of the substance under study react in a uniform and predictable way. What is actually observed is the behavior pattern of a considerably large number of these particles. If we believe in the principles of quantum mechanics it is really not possible to have absolute uniformity in the microcosm. This modern view of matter tells us that one of its chief attributes is randomness. Nature is essentially random though some general patterns allow the human interpretation that results in the formulation of the so-called laws of nature. So any analysis of what is happening in a laboratory experiment has to be communicated and formulated in terms of what really are statistical symbols which will prove valuable in the macrocosm in dealing practically with the reactions that were observed and in predicting similar behavior in the future. The symbols and myths of science find companion symbols and myths in the language of theology. Both endeavors deal with areas that lie essentially on the borderline of our direct consciousness.

Just what is a symbol? It is a kind of sign. A sign is any reality which, when known, or when entering into our consciousness, leads to the knowledge of another reality apart from it, of which it is seen as the sign. Thus when we see smoke, we can immediately conclude that associated with it there is fire. This is a natural sign. Or when we see the character # we know that it means "number," or & we know that it means "and." These are arbitrary signs, or those which become signs because of human agreement. Sometimes these arbitrary or conventional signs are very necessary for our well being — as is the case with a traffic signal, or stop sign, or the diamond-shaped yellow sign which indicates that we are coming upon a curve in the road ahead. Most of us become so familiar with the phenomenon of signs that we take them for granted.

As we said, a symbol is a sign, but not all signs are symbols, nor can some signs even become symbols. A symbol is a very special kind of sign. It is a sign that is used in certain circumstances or conditions of human intercourse to take the place of the thing that it is a sign of. It substitutes for the thing signified. It is a kind of logical and emotional "stand-in" for what it represents. Thus a road sign can never become a symbol because we cannot think of any circumstance of human inter-relationships where it could be used to take the place of what it points out, say, a curve in the road.

On the other hand a sign that is able to, and has become a symbol, is the flag of the United States of America. In international commerce it is recognized as a sign, the sign of this country. On the high seas the captain of a foreign vessel, seeing the American flag displayed on a ship whose identity he is trying to establish, would come immediately to the knowledge that the ship is one sailing under American registry. No one would doubt that in this circumstance the flag is definitely a sign.

But in another context it can also become a symbol. It can take the place of what it represents. Imagine a situation in Rome, Italy, where members of the Red Brigade spit upon it, tear it to pieces and burn the remnants. While we might be angry to hear this, we would not consider it to be either an insane or meaningless action. Or take the more comfortable scene where, at the beginning of a baseball or football game, the flag is slowly raised on a mast in a prominent position on the field, the national anthem is played and sung and people stand at attention — many with lumps of pride in their throats, overwhelmed with a feeling of patriotism. No one would say that this is insane or meaningless — that it is crazy to feel this way about a piece of cloth imprinted with a red, white and blue pattern. Here the flag is a symbol: it is taking the place of the reality it represents: the American way of life, the American system, the American government or whatever. The emotion that would be directed to that American value is now directed to its symbol. This process is called cathexis.

For a symbol to be truly effective it must be cathected. The emotion or value associated with the reality it is a sign of must be transferred to the sign. Psychologically this process is referred to as displacement. We know that there are unhealthy displacements of psychic energy from one object or person to another, as when because of a bad experience with one teacher, a student expresses a dislike for all teachers. Such displacement evidences the beginning of a prejudice. But in the case of the special kind of displacement that cathexis is, the transfer is not considered to be at all harmful, because such transfers occur with the blessing and understanding of the society or culture in which they take place. If the culture is wholesome, the transfer will be healthy and allow release of psychic energy that otherwise would not have been possible. Cathexis is so commonplace that we scarcely give it a second thought, but simply take it for granted. We do not consider it harmful, but beneficial, in the course of human events.

Thus to the pygmy in the Ituri forest in the heart of Africa the reality of our flag in all its naked splendor will be revealed. He sees it for what it actually is, and might well conclude that since it is made of excellent material, displaying sharp and flashy colors, it would make a fine loincloth. All the girls in the village would be impressed. To this pygmy the flag is neither a symbol nor even a sign; it is just a piece of cloth.

The sea captain views the flag as a sign revealing to him a ship of American registry. The patriotic American at opening ceremonies in a football game, however, experiences the flag as a symbol, cathected for him with all the emotion that he attaches to the American way of life, to the country that is his fatherland which he treasures with all his heart.

In ritual and ceremony cathexis implies a transfer of emotion. But in the symbolism of science, mathematics, language, philosophy and theology cathexis refers to values or significance rather than emotion. The meaning or valence of the thing signified is attributed to the sign. So what is involved is an intellectual rather than an emotional appreciation of the symbol in its relationship to what it symbolizes.

I do not have to emphasize how important symbols are in religious cult and in theology as well as in science. We genuflect to, bow our heads to, and kiss the crucifixes in our churches. We venerate the statues, pictures and other images of Christ and the saints. The sacramental system that we cherish is replete with deep symbolic significance. But many people do not think that the sacraments are as well appreciated today as they were in the past. Undoubtedly we can assign a loss of cathexis as the reason for this perception. The emotional response that was once evoked from sacramental rituals — and to a certain extent by images and other appurtenances in the Church — does not seem to be evident among worshipers today. One area, though, where cathexis seems to remain strong and viable is that of the eucharistic liturgy. Many still feel and respond to the real presence of Jesus in the eucharistic elements.

Another area where cathexis survives is in the sacrament of baptism, and this despite or maybe because of the fact that there has been a misinterpretation of the symbolism as originally intended. For us today water is used in cleansing. So the use of water in baptism would signify for us the purification of a person, the spiritual washing away of his sins. But we know that water, in the estimation of ancients, best symbolized life and death. In the rather arid lands where baptism first achieved this significance water could indeed be a matter of life and death. A refreshing cup of water revitalized the weary pilgrim traversing dusty desert roads. The Hebrew scriptures told the story of how all life began in the water — and this idea is not so far removed from our opinion today. Their teaching about the beginning was reflected in the experience of all who had anything to do with conception and birth. The life of the individual human being and animal, too, people thought, begins in water. They did not appreciate venereal fluids or the *liquor amnii* as anything much more than a kind of water. On the other hand, water could signify death for a person who does not know how to swim, and few in that environment did. To be immersed in water is tantamount to death. The story of the great flood in Scripture amply demonstrated the lethal potential of too much water. This story is also contained in the Gilgamesh epic of the Babylonians.

For the Hebrew the cloud was a symbol of Yahweh. As he led his people through the desert Yahweh appeared to them during the day as a cloud; his presence in the holy of holies was marked by a cloud. The cloud represented the waters that exist in the empyrean reaches above the earth where God dwells. His power over life and death is in the clouds. If he does not send rain or if he lets loose a flood, people die. If he sends the gentle rain it promotes life and provides refreshment. Today all of this is lost on us. Though we still reverence and appreciate the sacrament of baptism, we do not see it as a means of identifying with the death and rising to a new life of Jesus the Lord, of participating in the paschal mystery of the new covenant, but rather as a vehicle for the cleansing of us from our sinful condition.

In sacramental symbolism there has been an even

more startling development in the case of the sacrament that we call confirmation. Originally it was part of the baptismal ritual itself. Even today it is anticipated in an anointing that takes place after the water is poured and the baptismal formula is pronounced. Like confirmation, it consists in an anointing with the oil called chrism. But the actual sacrament of confirmation in the Western Church is reserved for a later time. This baptismal anointing is only ceremonial in nature.

In the early Church, as today, two kinds of ritual oil were employed. The first was an oil that was extracted from olives. It was an oil that was seen as a rich source of energy. It was used, as it is today in some countries, in the preparation of food. It also supplied fuel for lamps and heaters in the ancient world. But it was also considered to be a strengthening oil when applied to the bodies of human beings. Since it was so rich, it provided instant strength. So it was used by athletes before they entered a competition or contest. People knew that it would not be helpful for competitors to eat a large meal before entering the arena. It could provide energy, but only very slowly; in fact, it produced sluggishness and cramps in some cases. But the ancients thought that olive oil applied to the muscles before the contest would produce the quick energy needed. They tried to work it into the skin by massage. They had no real idea of the relative impenetrability of the various layers of skin that we moderns have. But even today are not ointments sold that advertising suggests might be helpful in dispelling viruses causing congestion from the lungs?

So the ancients rubbed olive oil into the muscles of an athlete, as they believed, to strengthen them before the contest. This idea was incorporated as symbol in the baptismal ceremony of the early Church. After all what greater contest is there than that with the forces of evil? What greater opponent does one have than one's own sinful self? When one is faced with making a commitment to accept one's death, to pay the penalty of sin, and to rise to a new life, free from the trammels of the flesh, the world and the devil, one needs great strength. Yet baptism for the ancient Church implied all of this. It was most appropriate, then, before the actual baptismal act to confirm the candidate, to strengthen him or her for the great symbolic ordeal. So olive oil, the oil of athletes, the strengthening oil was used to confirm them in their intention. As for the baptismal ceremony itself the men were separated from the women, for just as they went down naked into the pool of water to be baptized by the deacons and deaconesses, now their whole naked bodies were anointed by the confirming oil by those same deacons and deaconesses in separate areas. They all believed that the oil of the Lord would give them strength symbolically to die with Christ and rise again to a new life, that it would confirm them in their desire to live as Christ lived.

The other oil used in the early Church was chrism. In Greek the oil itself was called *myron;*

chrism or Christ-oil was the designation given to it when it was used symbolically in the baptismal ceremony. The ceremony of using this oil was called chrismation in the Eastern Church and in the Western Church christening, signing, or simply the sign.

After the separate baptism of the men and the women by the deacons and deaconesses, all were clothed in white garments and met in an assembly before the presiding priest or bishop. Chrism or Christ-oil was then poured by him over the head of each to symbolize the baptized person's identity with Christ, the Messiah, the one who was thought to have himself been anointed with this kind of oil. The baptized thus became other Christs, other Messiahs, other persons anointed to accomplish the same task that Jesus had undertaken.

Myron was an oil concocted from ingredients taken from pine trees. It was widely used in ancient times as a kind of deodorant. Its piney scent masked body odors. The ancient world did not know aluminum chlorhydrate, so they could not suppress the flow of sweat. But they could overcome its odor with a more pungent one. It seemed highly desirable for all of those who served in some kind of public role, who were significant ministers or servants of the people exercising some public commission on their behalf to use this oil while they performed their duties. Or if they did not, it was at least symbolically important for them at the time of their inauguration into their task to have this oil poured over them to signify that their lives and activities in the service of the public ought to be redolent with sweetness and good repute. So the oil was used in this ritual way with kings, priests and prophets. It was ill-becoming these important officials and spokespersons to live in a bad odor. They must make a good impression on people to carry out their mission effectively.

The Hebrew word "messiah" means one who has been anointed — with *myron* or a similar oil, of course. The Greek word "christos" from which we get our word "Christ" means the same thing. ("Christ" was not, as some people think, the last name of Jesus; that would have been Bar-Joseph; the word "Christ" is an epithet designating his appointment to perform his salvific mission among men.)

Thus it is that in baptism every Christian is reminded also of the mission each one has to work toward salvation and to minister to others in achieving that same goal. Christ and the Christian have the same essential task; as they have both celebrated the paschal mystery, so they must work together, they must both perform the same task of the salvation of the world.

When infant baptism became the regular thing in all communities a number of changes were introduced into the ritual of the sacrament. It was seen that an infant could not make the faith commitment that baptism demanded. His or her sponsors had to do that; but it was appropriate that when the person baptized reached such a stage of maturity that the commitment to the Christian way of life could be appreciated, some ritual affirmation of it was in order. The person baptized had to publicly say "yes" to the action taken by sponsors years before on his or her behalf. The christening with oil that had taken place in earlier times at the close of the baptismal ceremonial seemed well-suited to this purpose. So it was that at a still later time chrismation or christening came to be recognized as a separate sacrament. But since it was a kind of confirmation of baptismal promises, this new name was given to it. And in the course of history it became the person who was confirmed, not the promises. So this sacrament underwent a complete symbolic metamorphosis.

In the mind of many the word "myth" is apt to conjure up the notion of a fairytale, or a story which, though perhaps entertaining, or even significant in illumining the human condition, contains not a shred of truth — if by truth one means the conformity of mental images to external reality. Stories about gods and goddesses in the ancient world are called myths, and they pretty well fit this definition. There is, however, a more technical sense in which the word "myth" is employed in theology today. To maintain clarity it would be better to employ the word "fable" to designate stories about gods and goddesses, fairytales, and other narrative which is useful both to entertain and shed some light upon the vagaries and caprices of human nature, but which does not pretend to be totally in conformity with what the contemporary world perceives as real. Then again, the word "legend" should be applied to tales which are not literally true, if truth means historically verifiable fact, but true in the sense that they do reflect the spirit of a person, an event or a particular era. A legend can supply for missing historical data; it can bridge over lacunae in an historical narrative, and be appreciated as quite fitting, if not strictly verifiable. So we have the story of George Washington and the cutting down of the cherry tree; I think it would be best classified as a legend.

Modern scripture research tells us that the infancy narratives as we have them in the Gospels can be considered largely as legends. Material for them was borrowed from the Old Testament and other sources, but they do fit quite well the idea that the Christian community had about the early days of Jesus. So they might be termed legends in the technical sense.

When the word "myth" is used in its technical sense it refers to a reality that does really exist in some way — but in a world of which we cannot be directly conscious. It does deal with truth — but not with reality as we are able to recognize it, verify it and deal with it in the world in which our consciousness dwells most comfortably. Mythology treats of a foreign kind of reality, one we cannot be familiar with, because we are not directly conscious of it, and it does not fit well the categories we have chiseled out in our minds to handle the data of the world of which we are directly conscious. It is truth about the reality of another system, one radically different from ours. Rudolf Bultmann has given us the classical definition of myth: the objectification in our world of the reality of another world of which we cannot be directly conscious.

Symbols and myths are related. Myths are often made up of a congeries of symbols. Categorization of myths becomes possible through an identification of the symbols contained. There are religious myths, scientific myths and a host of others — recognizable as such from the type of symbols employed.

We recognize the creation myth related in the first chapter of the book of Genesis as a religious myth. God is the principal actor. Not only he but his creative action belong to another world. Never in our world do we experience something being made from nothing. No human being was present to verify what took place — and if one were present he could not have identified what took place precisely as creation: he would have witnessed only origins. What actually took place is revealed to us from the other world in which it chiefly occurred, and its effects are described so that the action itself can be objectified in our world.

We may take umbrage at the use of the term, but religious myths are really no strangers to us; the Bible is filled with them. But if we apply the term to the world of science, it becomes even more difficult to see. For science prides itself in dealing with the realities of our world. How then can there be a scientific mythology? Yet really just a little reflection will manifest to us that, whether we go to the macrocosm, the vast reaches of the universe with its billions of galaxies, or the microcosm, the world of atomic nuclei and electrons, we are projecting our consciousness into areas with which it has no complete and direct contact — areas where realities exist that are largely unverifiable by the kind of laboratory research that would give us absolute reassurance that we are indeed dealing with the truth of *our* world.

Maybe we would be reluctant to call the famous formula of Einstein about the equivalence of mass and energy a myth. If anything seems certain it is that $E = mc^2$. The effects of this formulation are known in the vast power of the fission and fusion bombs. They are felt in an even more practical way in the nuclear reactors that are providing the electrical energy we need for our homes and industry. Yet scientific fact by its very definition has to be empirically verifiable. The equation $E = mc^2$ is not. It is merely a formula for capturing in the world of our consciousness the reality of the world of subatomic physics, of which we can in no way be directly conscious. It is a myth in the fullest sense. Statistically speaking, it is true; absolutely speaking it is not verifiable and therefore cannot be held as scientifically established as true. Nowhere have the human senses or the instruments they can employ witnessed the total transformation in the microcosm of atomic mass into pure energy. In fact, can we really verify, independently of any interference our measuring sticks might inject into the formulation, that what we know as mass and energy in the macrocosm really exist in the interior of the atom?

Do we not have to resort to the overtly mythological world of quantum mechanics to account for anything that occurs at this level of reality?

When we move away from the familiar Euclidian geometry where parallel lines never meet and the angles of a triangle add up to 180° and approach Riemannian formulations about curved space where parallel lines are bound to meet and the angles of a triangle add up to 270° we are distancing ourselves from the world of our direct consciousness. We are moving into myth.

When we enter the world of quantum mechanics we feel even more like Alice in Wonderland. But of course our consciousness will not even let us enter that land. It can be dealt with only in myth. For quantum mechanics does not deal with anything objective at all. It would be absolutely meaningless to speak, as we do in our world, of a particle at rest at a given point in space whose presence could be verified. The world of quantum mechanics is a totally indeterminate world; its chief characteristic is randomness; its laws are only statistical generalizations bringing into our consciousness what must lie always totally beyond it. Its cornerstone is Werner Heisenberg's principle of indeterminacy which states that there can never be any simultaneous verification of the location and momentum of any particle: ($\Delta q \times \Delta p \approx h$). If the location of a particle is known for certain ($\Delta q = 0$), then its momentum could never be known definitely, for it would have to be infinity. Moreover, in this system reality has to be partially created by both the measuring rod and the observer. If we set up an experiment to mark the passage of an electron as a particle, the experiment will reveal that the electron indeed does have the characteristics of a particle. But if in another experiment we let the electron be what it "wants" to be, it will appear as a wave.

So physics has developed a definite mythology of its own — quite an esoteric one at that. A number of years ago there seemed to be some semblance of respectability maintained by dealing with Greek letter particles, with names that seemed to be truly scientific and in no way mythological. But now an endless host of hadrons have been broken down into quarks. And quarks come in at least five, and very probably six flavors. They are colored and are held together by gluons. All matter is ultimately made up of five (and probably six, though the last one has not been discovered as yet at this writing) quarks, six leptons and four gluons or forces. And what are the names of the quarks that have been discovered to date? Up, down, strange, charm and bottom! And there probably is a top!

Is this mythological language or is it not? Where indeed does the word "quark" come from? Is it a Greek word meaning "ultimate"? No, it is an ersatz word found in one of the novels of James Joyce.

No doubt the quaint names designate some reality. The bubble chambers of our great synchro-cyclotrons give evidence of that fact; there each particle or event has a way of announcing its presence in the mass spectrometer, electret and other detectors. It is how these phenomena are translated into the realm of our consciousness that is fascinating. Only mythology can accomplish it.

So that science on which ultimately all other science rests, physics, must allow for mythological formulations and understandings. Otherwise the seemingly irreconcilable opposites with which one has to deal can never be reconciled in conscious activity where reconciled they must be if they are to be accepted and dealt with. For as Claude Lévi-Strauss indicates, only myths can harmonize irreconcilable opposites.

We know that myths cannot really be manufactured; they have to be discovered. Both myths and symbols may initially resist any kind of arbitrary imposition on society They may be proposed and eventually confirmed and accepted, but quite often they arise in a seemingly spontaneous way in a culture, usually over long periods of time, from the not-too-easily explored areas of that culture's consciousness and experience. They often correspond in no common way to the archetypal images that dominate the concerns and values of the culture.

Some symbols, such as mathematical ones, seem to apply universally. Such mythological realities as absurd numbers, the idea of infinity and tesseracts can be dealt with only in mathematical symbolism. So, too, many religious myths and symbols seem to be universally accepted, and various world religions provide for them. Unlike mathematical symbols, religious ones are often imprecise and vague. Many are highly subjective in their interpretation and application; a symbol that lies at the very roots of the religiosity of one person will rest on the periphery of another person's religious consciousness. But many religious symbols are still indigenous to particular cultures or ethnic groups. There can be no positive knowledge of God in Buddhism; the only fully respectful attitude is that of "no-mind." Christianity has its Trinity. Islam is broad-minded in recalling the prophets. Hinduism has its evil as well as its good gods.

What symbols and myths accomplish universally is to bring us into a new presence, a presence that is often awesome and mysterious.

We often speak of presence in terms of space and time. What is not distant from us, what is not removed from us in either area is what is present to us. Presence is looked upon objectively. It is not usually seen as something I create. What is there is present to me. Yet a brief reflection will bring us to the realization that presence is indeed something that I create. Things are not just present to me. I render them present by focusing my attention upon them. Presence is a kind of feeling of contact with an outside reality rendered in terms of some aspect of the self-reflective consciousness. Prompted by myths and symbols, my self-reflective consciousness can render present to me the fantastic realities of a world that lies far beyond my immediate experience, a world of science or a world of religious truth.

If people today feel the absence of God or religious reality in their lives, it is partially because those who minister to them have lost their feeling for or ability to deal with religious symbolism. There can be no feeling or creation of a religious presence without appropriate symbols, credible symbols, to excite the self-reflective consciousness. And credible symbols are those that do not conflict with other well-established ones.

Think of the effective pastoral use of symbolism in by-gone eras. Gabriel Vahanian, in his book *Wait Without Idols,* studies Herman Melville's *Moby Dick* at some length. The Melville story is fraught with religious symbolism and mythology — symbolism and mythology that are geared to the era and locale of the story. Of particular interest is the chapel in the East Coast whaling village out of which Captain Ahab operated. The pastor, who was a former sailor and harpooner, had the chapel outfitted like a ship. On the wall was a great sea-scape depicting a ship tossed about by monstrous waves and yet showing the sun breaking through the clouds. When, as Vahanian says, the pastor delivers his sermon, it is appropriately on Jonah, and he pictures the whole world like a ship on its dangerous passage out. Thus the symbolic context of the whole religious enterprise in this village was the very life that persons who worshipped in this chapel lived.

Obviously such rich symbolism is not readily forthcoming today in urban parishes where vastly different groups of people congregate for worship. The lack of uniformity in occupation and interest is one of the big problems that stands in the way of

meaningful religious symbolism. But even if no one
can inculcate such a deep-seated religious symbolism in our churches today, a symbolism such as
was encountered in that New England village, at
least a symbolism which bears some meaning for
their existence in today's scientific and technological world can be provided for our parishioners,
more and more of whom, as time passes on, are
becoming involved in science and technology.

In the following chapters we shall explore some
of that scientific symbolism as it is applied to the
various traditional sectors of theology.

Chapter III

GOD

THE outstanding characteristic of the contemporary theology of God is its anthropotropism, that is, its humanistic inclination, its being bent toward man. Past theologies, especially Protestant ones, have been especially theotropic, that is, emphasizing the power and majesty of God, being bent toward God.

Man is a curious animal. He has always manifested an interest in penetrating the mysteries of God. He wants to seek God out in his own realm, to invade heaven itself to find out what God is really like. Traditional theology has taught that the purpose of creation is to give honor and glory to God. God is the be-all and end-all of everything. God gives meaning and purpose to human existence. Without God man is at sea. Without God the answer to man's perennial question, "What's it all about?" would have to be, "I don't know." Man needs God. The tendency of human kind is to violate the Protestant principle and make God a means to an end. It takes an heroic effort — no doubt impossible without the assistance of grace — to let God be God, and not subject him to human purposes. But this ideal must always be set before man. The highest act he could perform would be to contemplate God in all his majesty and glory and express in respectful worship and jubilant song that God is beyond and above all, yet has condescended to enable man to become his obedient servant. Past theology has been absorbed in the other-worldly.

By contrast, today's theology seems almost totally secular. Karl Marx called the attention of the world to the fact that it was not true to itself: it was devoting entirely too much attention to the other-worldly. Religion, because of its total preoccupation with God, was neglecting mankind. Christianity was supposed to bring attention to bear on the poor, the downtrodden, the outcast, and do something about them. But in reality all that it could offer them was to look forward to some better life in another, future world. Thus it was no better than the ancient religions that it replaced. All the Christian religion could really promise to deliver was "pie in the sky." Instead of helping, all Christianity was doing was abetting man's neglect of his fellowman here on earth. The doctrine that man is the very image of God, that the second of the great commandments inculcates love for neighbor similar to that paid to God himself failed to exercise as much influence on the spirituality of the past as the doctrine that man ought to work out his salvation by focusing his attention on God and asking his help in observing the law that he gave to mankind. People were told that they must, for the sake of God and in imitation of Christ, bear up under suffering, endure abject poverty, sustain oppression and welcome difficulties in order to gain a higher place in heaven.

Contemporary theologians have taken Marx's challenge very seriously. They have tried to re-focus the attention of believers upon man. In doing this, they felt, they have not turned their back upon God, for man is the image of God, and one cannot really know anything about God except in human terms. This focus of attention upon man has been the watershed dividing the contemporary theological enterprise from that of the past. If the theology of yesteryear defined the very purpose of human existence in terms of God, that man exists to give glory to God, then the new theology re-defines it in terms of man himself. Gregory Baum captures the true *Geist* of the current view when he states that God's glory indeed is man fully alive. This kind of turnabout is typical. If man exists to glorify God, and God's glory is situated in man, man exists for himself.

Needless to say, this new "manwards" orientation of theology has raised great problems. What has become of the Protestant principle, that principle which resists making God an idol, making him a means to an end, making him exist for the sake of humanity? Humans must always be subservient to God, not God to humans. Modern theology seems to have overturned this idea. God is made a means to an end. He has become no more than an idol. If theologians would not go as far as to say that God exists for the solace and convenience of humanity, at least they seem to teach that he exists as a challenge to humans, to draw out humanity to a more mature status, to a condition of loving concern such as he manifests, to make humanity his vicar in moving the world to a better state. Catholic theologians too have winced at the excessive anthropotropism of some of their conferres. No less than their Protestant counterparts do they resist suborning God.

A subtle temptation that is inherent in theology's new outlook on God is to make humanity self-sufficient. There is no doubt that current scientific and technological development has contributed immensely to this persuasion. More and more humanity is coming to see itself in charge of the world that formerly was entrusted to the provident care of God. Gradually humanity is taking over responsibility for the earth. Our ability largely to master our environment has given us confidence. The modern world is growing into a preoccupation with ecology. There is more concern for the future of humanity itself. That future may, with the help of recent technological developments in the area of genetic engineering and evolutionary planning, be open to better possibilities for humanity: the elimination of birth defects, control of disease, and refurbishment of the means of sustenance. We may no longer have to rely on God to assure a happy outcome for the future. We can provide it for ourselves, and this thought may even lead us to wonder if we ought not to assert our independence of God — even whether we were created by God. The contemporary *causa sui* project of humanity, as Gogarten has termed it, has forced a drastic reconsideration of the theology of God. And it has been largely the result of humanity's contemplation of its own scientific and technological prowess.

This new mood that has descended upon theology in our day has been enfleshed in a very wide range of practical viewpoints encompassing on the one hand the most radical theology — Oresteanism, or death of God theology — and on the other the rather mild suggestion that God has become more involved with humanity today than he ever was before. But almost every theology, radical or conservative, has felt the impact of the new thrust toward the experiential. Older theologies were very comfortable in the ambit of metaphysics. Faith and reason was the catchcall: faith seeking reason and reason seeking faith. This intellectual approach to God has not been totally relegated to the dust bin, but its influence is felt less today than in the past, because religious experience has become the starting point of almost all viable theological speculation in our time. If theological language is still relevant today, it is because it best suits a significant segment of our experience. Since the time of William James' famous essay even scientists have acknowledged the fact that religious experience is a unique and distinct type of human experience, that it differs substantially from every other kind of experience and must stand on its own right. Surveys have shown that upwards of 40 percent of the population have at least once in their lives been in the spell of an overpowering spiritual force which corresponds to their notion of the divinity, at least in some vague way. About half of these have had such experiences more than once. A few report that they have them frequently. Most have never discussed them with anyone else; they show much resistance in reporting them to or discussing them with a clergyman. They consider them to have more cognitive than sentient content. Some feel that these experiences are triggered by other events, not excluding sexual intercourse. When, of course, experiences like these are taken into account by theologians, when strictly rational theology is squared off against experiences like these, an automatic opening is created for an interface with science. For the scientist is interested in interpreting human experience of all kinds.

Based more on the experience of society at large than that of any individual, responding to the radically secular mood of the times as we described it in the first chapter, Oresteanism, Theothanatism, or the death of God theology, though never popular, has titillated the minds of theologians in the second half of the century. It was a distinctive American contribution, but it was a flash in the pan.

Thomas J. J. Altizer, the best known proponent of Oresteanism, taught that the transcendent God of Christ, the God of Judaeo-Christian literature, died when Jesus died on the cross. The modern secular mood and spirit evidence the fact that the once transcendent God, the God whom Christ acknowledged as his Father, has now become a purely immanent God. Altizer describes the death of God in terms of the Hegelian synthesis. At one time people struggled with the problem of the simultaneous transcendence and immanence of God. How could God be infinitely above us, infinitely distant from us, and at the same time so close to us? How can he be both creator and father? How can he be both master and lover? This thesis and antithesis, so vexatious in theology, has now been synthesized in favor of a totally immanent God: humanity is its own god.

For William Hamilton, too, God is literally dead. Today's literature betrays a radically secular mood. The fact is that because of his scientific and technological progress humanity no longer has to rely on God. It can get along very well, and maybe even better without him. God is seen to have no function in the modern world. Those who honestly confront this problem will refuse to create another kind of God, or make the God they know a kind of idol in the modern world; they will not relegate him to the status of a sop to satisfy human desires and longings; they will rather let him die. And the death of God is not an altogether bad thing. Once God is eliminated from the human scene, we are thrown back on our own; we are challenged freely to assume responsibility for our own development and the care of the world in which we live. We are really freer now to be ourselves than if we had to contend with and rely on a God.

Paul Van Buren develops this idea even more fully. Even though God is dead — and maybe even because God is dead — Jesus assumes a greater importance in the lives of Christians. The real

meaning of the Gospel and the ultimate values it inculcates must be related to the all-important issue
of human freedom. The message of Jesus tells us
that we have to be free — even of God himself. One
must live completely open and free the way that
Jesus did. What one has called God is no more than
the ultimate value that one sees in life. For today's
world that value has to be human freedom.

Gabriel Vahanian is the least radical of the Theothanatists. He maintains that God is not literally
dead, but silent in the modern world. It is as if he
were dead. What really is dead are the old, time-
worn, useless religious forms and theological
formulations. God lies dormant waiting for a new
human contact which has to be made without making him an idol or subjecting him as an object to
human use or benefit. Only when some great leader
or prophet arises once again to proclaim effectively
the Protestant principle will God come alive again
in society.

While this kind of theology has flabbergasted,
amazed, amused, intrigued and perhaps even challenged the theological community, it seems to have
affected popular piety minimally, if at all. Believers
cannot live without God. So the idea that God is
dead was largely rejected as nonsense by the
Church and by the ordinary person in the pews. But
it titillated the theologians, and made them aware
of what might be the ultimate consequences of an
anthropotropic approach to God.

The Jewish Theothanatist Rabbi Richard L.
Rubenstein might have had higher hopes not only

that his theology would be a reflection of the culture of the community, but that it would be assimilated by the Jewish people. He recalls the murder by the Nazis of six million Jews. He asks a hard question: has this action not refuted once and for all the two foundational beliefs of Judaism: that God is the Lord and Master of history, and that he has a special relationship to the Jewish people? And if this question must be answered in the affirmative, then is it not appropriate to say that the God who once revealed himself to Israel, announced to them that they were his special people, stood by them and led them to victory in their time of trial in the past, is now dead?

So often in the past, theology has responded to the challenge of culture simply by assimilating it, by incorporating it in some way or other into its own fabric. The Theothanatists have hoped that this would become evident in their case; that it would be clear that Oresteanism was simply a theology that is able fully to introject the prevalent secular mood that is a result of the scientific and technological progress of modern times. But some commentators have opined that death of God theology has not really incorporated the secular mood; it has simply succumbed to it. The death of God really marks the death of theology itself. Theothanatism offers no exit to the basic problem of our culture.

Philosophy, too, has been challenged by the secular *Geist*. Marxism has had its impact in this area as well as upon theology. A definitely anthro-

potropic philosophy has resulted, one that is seen
as able to serve theology in these times as well.
Because it is orientated toward human concerns,
existentialism has been employed extensively in the
acculturation of Christian belief today. Existentialism has influenced a wide range of theological
speculation, from the biblical interpretations of
Rudolf Bultmann and the systematic investigations
of Paul Tillich, to the ethical considerations of
James Gustafson and Paul Ramsey. The prominent
Roman Catholic systematic theologian Karl Rahner
is taken with the existentialism of Heidegger,
although to the extent he can, he still clings to some
of the fundamental principles of Scholasticism.

Existentialism is not a single organized philosophical system like Scholasticism or Kantianism,
but a loose grouping together of a number of as-
sumptions about human existence. Only humans,
of all creatures, have to face the question of being.
In fact, humanity can be defined as the reality for
whom being becomes an issue. Only humanity can
separate itself from its being, question it and do
something about it. The human being is uniquely
such that it is never fully possessed. It is rather a being to be achieved. Human reality is most appropriately described by the German word *Dasein*. Humanity is being-there, located being, being for
which there is a beyond; humanity's being is a projected being; its proper place is out in front of
itself. Existentialists distinguish two kinds of being
in humans: a being they have in common with other
beings in virtue of which humanity is simply what it

is; and a being-to-be-made, a projected being whereby humanity can become what it wants to make of itself. It is this latter which sets apart human reality from all other.

Being human essentially implies the power to transcend, to bring the actual locus of our being to the projected locus. To be what we really are, humanity must be constantly other to itself. Transcendence is achieved only through a never-ending investment of one's being in freely chosen projects. By reason of its free will humanity has the power fully to dispose of itself within the limits of its located being. An individual's personality phenomenologically is perceived by others as the sum total of all his projects achieved or to be achieved. His personhood is noted by others in terms of the way he has made use of his freedom. In a word, any human being can be apprehended as the congeries of the ways in which he or she has chosen to exist. One does not say that the human being just is, he or she must exist. The very word "exist" comes from Greek words that imply standing out from oneself. To exist, humanity must continually transcend what it is.

In considering what this philosophy implies one is reminded of a statement attributed first to Cardinal Nicholas of Cusa and reiterated in later times by Pico della Mirandola in his invective against Aristotle: "The nature of God is to have no nature!" The existentialist theologian sees humanity as imaging God in the fact that it, too, has no fixed nature. Through its free choices humanity, like God, makes itself what it wants to be. But at times, in the theology influenced by existentialism, one encounters a tendency to judge the importance of God for humanity from his helpfulness in promoting true human existence, in assisting us to be free, to become what we really ought to be. And when this is the case, this perspective on God also violates the Protestant principle.

The Roman Catholic theologians Karl Rahner and Bernard Lonergan have proposed an approach to the theology of God that has been called transcendentalism. It is a potpourri, an amalgam to the extent that two opposites can be fused, of existentialist thought and the old classical Scholasticism. Like the existentialist they consider first of all the limit situations in human existence. To be true to itself humanity must transcend these limits. Lonergan and Rahner describe human limitation in terms of a kind of horizon.

An horizon is a maximum field of vision from a determinate standpoint. But humanity continuously experiences its capability of pushing back any horizon. As we walk along, the horizon recedes. Our ability to transcend seems almost unlimited. As long as we keep going, old horizons vanish and new ones arise to take their place. As is the case with human vision, so also with our intellectual faculty.

The basic horizons of human intellect for Lonergan fall initially into the categories of the known, the known unknown and the unknown unknown. Transcendence allows us to establish six differentiated worlds, those of the sacred and profane, common sense and theory, the interior and the exterior. Again transcendence leads to integration of these by a process of elimination, synthesis, oscillation, transposition or mediation. Rahner argues to a preconceptual absolute horizon which must serve as a ground for the questioning of being itself, and eventually for a transcendental method of reaching the divine. In the various horizons which a person encounters he becomes aware of the disclosure, first of all, of the possibility of transcendence itself, and through actual transcendence, finally, of the ultimately transcendent reality, of that which lies fully beyond human grasp and appears as the absolute and final horizon, beyond which there can be no more.

The transcendentalist approach to God is highly philosophical, but it, too, relies upon psychological and empirical analyses of the mechanisms of human knowledge, consciousness and experience. Much more than the intellectual avenue to the divine opened by St. Thomas Aquinas and the Scholastics, the approach favored by these theologians looks for support to science, and consequently has been appreciated by many as one that is quite viable in today's world.

Stemming from existentialist philosophy, scientific anthropology and recent psychological studies are many of the notions advanced by elpidian theologians, theologians of hope, like Wolfgang Pannenberg, Jürgen Moltmann and Johannes Metz. These theologians view transcendence in terms of promise, a promise for the future which affects the present social situation of humanity. If humanity is to transcend, we must learn to trust, to risk and even to revolt against our present state. It is only if the human, who is the only creature who can do so, can hope that he will be able to transcend the present and move toward a brighter future with whatever means becomes necessary. Hope may be defined as desire accompanied by a real expectation of obtaining what is desired. It is the belief that what one wants is really obtainable. Psychological studies have shown us that hope can be experienced very early in the history of the child. It seems to arise from childhood fantasies. The child is the only one who goes so far as to believe that what is really unobtainable can be reached. So from very early years hope enters as a structure of human life. It provides for a true definition of man as the only animal that can hope.

Held in the spell of anthropotropism, these theologians emphasize that God reveals himself in humanity. The only way we can come to know God in any adequate way is by looking at ourselves. True to their existentialist mentors, the elpidians propose that humans as humans are really a promise of something to come. Humanity as the reality that it is founds an ontology of the "not-yet" because of the way our lives are payed out. The past is gone. Before one can even think of the word "present" the present is gone. It is mercurial. It escapes immediately, so it is hardly real. The only thing that is left for us is the future. And that, without hope, can be uncertain.

Some of these theologians say that we must stop talking about the God who is, because this type of language has traditional metaphysical implications. We must turn our attention to the God who assures our future, the God of the absolute future. The historical process in which humanity recognizes it is involved must be grounded in something outside of itself if it is to be fully meaningful. The process has proven itself to be too shaky, too insecure, too volatile to be on firm footing. The ground of the process must lie at the end as its goal. The ground of history must lie in the future.

People today can no longer be guided by tradition, by the God who was. Much of this tradition can no longer be squared away with modern intellectual and scientific progress. Past theologies have become irrelevant because they were grounded in the consciousness of a divinity and its operations that are out of place in modern culture, that can no longer provide any hope for the future. Nor does thinking of God as present help, for as was said, the present supplies less security than even the past; it is continuously in flux. Humanity's only hope is to look to the God who guarantees the future, who has promised to be all in all.

For the elpidians Jesus serves as a prolepsis, an anticipation of what is to come. We see in Jesus the perfect human being, the man who is able to serve both God and his fellow-man with perfection.

Jesus is a man who loves deeply. If all human beings were like Jesus, the ideal society, the perfectly
functioning community of love, care and concern
could be realized. Even the Marxist philosopher
Ernst Bloch is intrigued by ideas such as these.
Would not such a community as envisioned by
these theologians be close to the Marxist ideal of
the classless society?

Elpidian theology undoubtedly has made its impact on the political theology of Johannes Metz as
well as the popular liberation theology. Not only
has liberation theology played an important role in
the social scene in Latin America, and to a certain
extent in the whole third world but it has in no common way captured the attention of theologians
everywhere. It would not be to our purpose here to
dwell upon it, both because it has been treated extensively elsewhere and especially because it does
not seem directly to stem from or be connected with
the current scientific view of humanity, but arises
rather from economic and social considerations.

The current theology of God which is most directly scientific in its methodology is one which
handles the issue of God and his meaning for
humanity in a positivist or empirical manner. At
first blush it might seem impossible to employ such
a methodology in treating of questions about God.
God cannot be the direct object of science or scientific study. We cannot put him in a laboratory, observe him and run him through a series of tests.
Even the mystics who have encountered God in the

most direct way possible in this life cannot provide
us with any information that could form a basis for
scientific analysis. What they have experienced, as
they will confess with great humility, is not God in
himself — that is quite impossible — but some kind
of emanation from God, some "touch" of God
which can leave its mark upon them. No, the object
of any empirical study of God cannot be God himself: it is rather God-talk. This approach to the
theology of God uses an analysis of religious
language and an assessment of its meaningfulness
for people today. In religious experience as well as
in other discernment situations traditional religious
language serves very well for both describing and
communicating what transpired. Scientific analysis
vindicates the validity of such language in conveying data and impressions from another world that
cannot be the direct object of human consciousness
in this world. With its symbolism and mythology
religion can cope where nothing else seems adequate.

The studies of theologians like Langdon Gilkey
have demonstrated that religious language continues to be meaningful even in today's secular society. What is passed over, because certainly it
cannot be the object of empirical research, is the
question of whether such language really has a ref-
erent. But the proponents of this methodology tell
us that it is not important whether what we call
God exists or not; what is significant for humanity
is that God-talk serves to illuminate certain other-

wise hidden aspects of human life, and affords a sense of ultimacy and meaningfulness that is definitely beneficial for human existence.

Akin to this approach is that of narrative theology. Theologians like John Shea are investigating story-telling as a vehicle for studying and communicating truths from another world. Religious language becomes meaningful because it can be used in stories to focus for man ultimate issues and values in his life.

Panentheism advances a most overtly scientific conceptualization of God. Panentheism must be carefully distinguished from pantheism. By pantheism is meant the formal identification of God with the whole or part of his creation. On the other hand, panentheism does not propose such a formal identity at all. It simply puts forth the idea that God is intricately involved in his creation; God is the ground of created being. The being, the operation and the direction of creatures has to be seated in God himself. God has to be intimately connected with what is going on in the world. To be involved in this way God has to be a process God.

The notion of God as the ground of his creation is not a new one at all. Paul had some such idea. He teaches us that it is in God that we live and move and have our being [Acts 17/28]. The word "panentheism" comes from three Greek words found in the Pauline corpus: *pan, en, theoi.* Everything exists in God.

Paul Tillich proposes that God is the ground of all being. It is he who sustains all creatures in their very existence; he keeps them from falling back into the nothingness that prevailed before creation. Roman Catholic theology traditionally sets forth a three-fold activity of God in relation to creation: he conserves all created reality in being, concurs with its movements, giving it the very ability to operate, and directs it to its goal through his providential care.

Something new and exciting, however, emerges from the modern concept of God as the ground of being. It is the notion of a God who, like his creation, is in process. God's involvement in creation is such that he shares with it this particular property. Not only is his activity bound up with the natural mechanical processes of the universe, but especially is he implicated in human history. The Bible pictures him in this way. When God's chosen ones suffer, he suffers; when they do evil, he is angry; when they observe his law and carry out his purposes, he rejoices. The God of Scripture does not resemble at all the God of the philosophers. Of course, metaphysicians would say that the God of revelation has to be an anthropomorphic God. This is to say that he has to appear and be described in fully human terms so that human beings can understand the message he is trying to convey. He has to look human so we can appreciate him. But really he does not change. Really he is not so involved. By using analogous language in this way Scripture is merely conveying to us in graphic terms one fact about God: he loves us and cares for us in his own way. But he really is no more immanent than transcendent, and his infinite transcendence demands that he be totally other to us.

But the modern theological tendency has taken this involvement of God with his creatures much more seriously. Modern theology seems ready to talk about a God who interacts with his creatures, particularly the ones that share with him an intellect and will. So it creates the seeming anomaly of a process God, a God who can change. And in this enterprise it looks to the leadership of a man who was not a theologian, but an expert mathematician and scientist, Alfred North Whitehead.

In his book *Process and Reality,* published back in 1929, Whitehead makes some challenging statements. It is as true to say that God is permanent and the world fluent as it is to say that the world is permanent and God is fluent. It is as true to say that God is one and the world many as it is to say that the world is one and God many. It is as true to say that in comparison with the world God is actual eminently as that in comparison with God that the world is actual eminently. It is as true to say that the world is immanent in God as it is to say that God is immanent in the world. It is as true to say that God transcends the world as that the world transcends God. It is as true to say that God creates the world as that the world creates God.

This kind of totally interlocking, reciprocal relativity might first seem to the theologian as being the worst type of heresy. But a more careful analysis of the propositions of Whitehead might reveal that there is a good deal of truth in his surmises. Could he just be saying that the modern world cannot comprehend a God who is completely aloof from his creation and its activity? Whatever knowledge we have of God has to be explicitated in terms of creatures. Only through the way of negation or analogy can we think or speak about God. In the negative way we take a perfection of a creature, deny any limits to it, and then apply it to God. Think of the power in a thunderstorm, expand it to the point where power is unlimited and call God omnipotent or all-powerful. Through the way of analogy a creature's perfection is applied to God with the understanding that God possesses a similar one, but in a much more perfect way. Thus we experience the care, concern and love of our earthly fathers and call God Father. When we call God immutable we try to preserve him from the change and corruption we experience among creatures. But the notion that change involves corruption is an ancient one. It may no longer be viable in today's world.

For the modern scientist a God who would be absolutely immutable would be an imperfect God. Immutability implies staticity. And a static God, a stagnant God, is hard to picture in the role of Creator of the amazing and marvelous energies of the universe. What is inert, what is not dynamic, what is not activated is not considered very valuable in the estimation of the modern mind. To be exciting and interesting, people as well as things have to be energized, active, dynamic. Nothing is as boring as a dull person. And it would be hard to picture God in this way.

It would be wrong to say that there is no fundament in traditional theology for saying that God is not inert, but totally energized, active and dynamic. The great thirteenth century theologian Thomas Aquinas describes God simply as *actus purus,* the one who is totally activated, pure action. There can be nothing that is not activated in God. There is no potency, no potential in him; everything is actual. In no way is he static or inert; he is full activity, completely energized. Whatever can be is in God.

How does this relate to the idea of immutability? Thomas Aquinas thought that God is both the *actus purus* and an immutable being. He saw no contradiction in this. Thomas felt that God had to be immutable, because whatever is perfect has to be unchangeable. If a reality changes, the Greek philosophy which has such an influence on him taught, it must either lose something that it had before, or gain something that it did not have before, and in either case it would at one time or another not be absolutely perfect. The Greeks had no concept of change without gain or loss — but then they did not know anything about quantum mechanics, either. The Greeks were strong on the idea of entropy, but weak on the idea of the conservation of mass/energy.

The great renaissance thinker, Cardinal Nicholas of Cusa, offers an idea through which we can arrive at a deeper and fuller understanding of how phenomena which we cannot reconcile on earth, in our dimensional system, can actually be realized in God, the infinite reality. Nicholas of Cusa is the only theologian I know who has attempted to describe the infinity of God in positive terms. Most other theologians have simply followed Thomas Aquinas and described God's infinity by using the negative way, that is, by taking some attribute of creatures with which we are familiar, applying it to God, but denying any limitation of it when it is applied to God. Experience tells us of the limitations of creatures. They have definite boundaries not only in space and time but in their very being itself. The Latin word *finis,* from which our word "finite" is derived signifies a boundary or limit. When we add to the word "finite" a negative proclitic "in-" we produce a word that signifies a reality that is in no way limited or restricted by boundaries; we arrive at a word that, we feel, adequately describes God as we would like him to be. Of course, it is impossible for us to have any completely positive conceptualization of the infinite. Even for mathematicians it has to be not a real but an ideal "number." We simply cannot squeeze the infinite into our finite minds. Infinity can only be a symbol. That symbol objectifies in our world the reality of another world of which we cannot be directly conscious; infinity can really exist only in another system outside of space-time. But Cardinal Nicholas of Cusa has come as close as anyone to describing infinity in positive terms. He states that the infinite is that reality that can encompass con-

traries within itself. Note that he does not say that
the infinite can reconcile contradictories; that
would be quite impossible; it can embrace only contraries. To ascertain the difference between contradictories and contraries we have to have recourse to
elemental logic.

Propositions which can neither be true together
nor false together are contradictories. So the statements "All grass is green," and "Some grass is not
green," are contradictories. If all grass is green then
it cannot be true that some grass is not green, and
contrariwise, if some grass is not green, then it cannot be true that all grass is green. But neither can
these two statements be false together. If it is false
that all grass is green and also false that some grass
is not green, the only conclusion we can draw is
that then there is no such thing as grass. On the
other hand, contraries are those propositions or
realities that cannot be true together, but which can
be false together. Thus the statements, "He is
standing," and "He is sitting," are contraries, not
contradictories. It is certainly true that if he is
standing he cannot at the very same time be sitting,
and contrariwise, if he is sitting, he cannot be
standing at the same time. These statements cannot
be true or realized together. But they can be false
together. If it is false that he is standing and false
that he is sitting, there is no problem. He may have
assumed another posture, like kneeling or lying
down. If he is kneeling it would be false that he is
standing and sitting.

If then in God's infinity contraries are compossible even in a positive sense, we could affirm of God that his standing is his sitting, his loving is his hating and his knowing is his willing.

It has always been amusing to me to observe how opposing sides in a conflict, whether that be war, racial strife, religious differences or just a game, can both appeal to God for support and victory, and how theologians could say that God loves both sides and treats them both with perfect equity. For finite beings it is never possible to put together contrary ideas, positions or activities. But if God is infinite, and what Nicholas of Cusa says is true, this is possible for God. Thus in one and the same act he can love the British and the Germans while they are at war, black people and white people engaged in racial strife, Baptists and Roman Catholics while they argue over the meaning of Scripture, and the Yanks and Dodgers while they are playing the world series. Human beings must be on one side or the other or reserve judgment. God can be on both sides at once.

If we define process as a series of activities, actions or operations, then there is no reason for saying that God could not be both immutable and in process. Immutability and changeableness would be contradictories. Immutability and process may be only at the most contraries. It might even be possible to consider God as being immutably in process. Only if process implies gain or loss would any difficulty arise. While it might well do so among finite beings, it does not seem necessarily to have to imply this in the infinite being.

Thus if we initiate a process, say to win $10,000 at a dice game, as the amount of our winnings increases we gain; as we begin to lose games, we suffer a loss. A process like this has to be thought of in terms of gain or loss. There can be no change in our status in this game without either gaining or losing. Suppose, though, that our goal is not $10,000, but an infinite amount of money (absurd though that may be). We have then entered a totally different world in which $10 is not further from the goal than $10,000. With respect to the infinite we have not really gained if we started with $10 and won $10,000. A googol ($10^{100}$, one with 100 zeros after it) or even a googolplex ($10^{10^{100}}$, a one with a googol of zeros after it, more zeroes than can be contained in the space in the known universe!) is no closer to infinity than a simple 1. In infinity nothing can be measured. There is no gain or loss. But this does not mean that there is no process. How is it possible to think of a Trinity of persons in God without recognizing some kind of process? How can the Son be generated and the Spirit be spirated if there is no process in the divine essence? Are not processions referred to when speaking of the origin of the Second and Third Persons in the Godhead? And what is a procession but the result of a process? And how can creation truly reflect God if he too is not in process?

Charles Hartshorne and Pierre Teilhard de Chardin are foremost among the panentheists who propose a process God. Both of them look to the involvement of God in what is going on in the universe to assure not only the evolution of higher and better forms but to guarantee also a happy outcome for the whole process. On the other hand, writers like Shubert Ogden, John Robinson and John J. Cobb expound a world-process that seems to be open-ended. The presence of God in the system does not guarantee a desirable effect. God's involvement does not preclude the possibility of deviation from hoped-for goals. God himself may not be able to avert a disaster.

Although the scientific data on which he based his studies would be out of date today, Pierre Teilhard de Chardin offers a good explanation of how a process God fits into and becomes an essential part of the process of evolution we witness in the development that has taken place in the world. What we apprehend as the energies of the universe is really the love of God. It is initially hidden from us and only gradually revealed. It is love that is drawing all the separate particles of matter, highly diffuse and separated at the Alpha point or beginning of the process, ultimately to a point of convergence which Teilhard calls Omega, that stage of the process where the whole conscious universe will be fully identified through Christ with the Creator. Divine love is explicitated in the universe in the form of radial energy, which is a centripetal force, drawing diverse elements of the universe toward a center. It operates in conjunction with tangential energy, which through a gradual process of entropization is being converted into radial energy. Tangential energy is a centrifugal force, which we see operational in a mechanical way among the various elements of the universe. Radial energy is basically the stuff of consciousness. All matter, even elemental atomic particles, possesses some minimum of radial energy, and consequently has some kind of rudimentary consciousness. But as separate atoms come together to form molecules, as molecules coalesce to from mega-molecules, as mega-molecules develop into living cells, as cells expand into organ systems and organs make up organisms, radial energy mounts and consciousness increases.

Thus far this process has gone through three quantum stages. Initially there was only the lithosphere, the world of inorganic matter. Then as radial energy in the system mounted, there emerged the biosphere, the realm of living things. Finally when, as Teilhard said, evolution became conscious of itself, when a self-conscious being, man, developed, the noosphere was born.

As we stated before, this scientific perspective is also a prophetic one. Not only does it offer a theory as to the rise of life and consciousness in the world, but it also integrates with it Paul's allusion to the fact that the time will come when Christ will become all in all. Initially Teilhard refers to the process that is on-going in the universe as "complexification," but eventually he reveals it as Christogenesis, that is the coming to maturity of the whole Christ, the mystical Christ. When Christ has attained to his fulness, then God will be all in all; his love will have suffused the whole universe and brought it to complete consciousness of himself.

By contemplating the verticils of new growth from stage to stage one should be able to predict with a good deal of certainty what the next quantum phase of conscious energy will comprise. By looking at the final period of the lithosphere, one would be able to discern the eventual emergence of the biosphere; and by examining the biosphere when it became ripe to give rise to something new, the noosphere could be predicted. So at present the verticils of the next quantum leap are in evidence, and what the next stage of consciousness will be can be ascertained. Teilhard himself does not use the term, but in line with his names for the other stages I would call the future development the hyperprosoponosphere.

In the hyperprosoponosphere human beings will lose their individuality, but not their personhood. It would be a condition of shared consciousness. We are separated from one another by our individuality not by personality. Personhood cannot develop except in a relationship with others. Deep involvement with others to the extent of sharing consciousness itself with them provides for the emergence of fully developed, mature personalities. But it suppresses what would isolate and divide: individuality. When consciousness is shared war, dissension and misunderstanding will disappear. Then humanity will be ready for its full identification with Christ. It will become with Jesus as its head the whole Christ. When the individuality that divides people and sets them at odds with one another passes away because of a shared consciousness, an ability intimately to understand and appreciate the standpoint of another, then a new, and the final, quantum of the earth's development will have been reached.

This highly imaginative and marvelous view, this unified vision gleaned from both scientific and theological sources, still stands as a challenge to us, and as a masterpiece of ingenuity and foresight for our times. Already, in this computer age, when the most recent advertising campaign seems to be one to put a computer in every home by the end of the millenium, a shared consciousness is becoming possible. In computers there is stored the best possible information about every facet and area of human knowledge and life. Here we have the shared consciousness and experience of the very best experts. As time goes on we will come to rely more and more upon this pooled consciousness, and less and less upon our own individual ideas.

It is interesting to note the fact that in one of the landings on the moon, our American astronauts relied not so much on their own visual observation, but rather on information that was stored in three computers, one on board and two earth-based. In this fashion they made a successful landing in a terrain they were not totally familiar with because they had not rehearsed on earth a landing at this particular spot, one they were forced to choose because of slight miscalculations of the landing vector.

As communication possibilities increase and the use of computers becomes more and more widespread, psychological introjection of the data contained in the storage areas of computers may well become possible, and a shared consciousness become a fact. The final stage of mankind envisioned by Teilhard will then have been reached.

One of Teilhard's key principles is the priority of radial energy over tangential energy. Radial energy guides and directs tangential energy to its own purposes. Conscious desire produces somatic evolutionary development. Look at a tiger. It is an almost perfect model of a predator. For short distances it is able to outrun its prey. With a tremendous leap it can position itself on its victim's back. With one blow from its powerful forepaw it can bring a deer or even a small buffalo down. Its claws, retracted while running, give it a good footing on the animal's back. Its sharp and long canines close on the victim's throat. Its dew claw extends to rip open the hide and expose the flesh. The tiger is perfectly equipped for the job of hunting it does. But Teilhard asks, "Which came first, the discovery that the tiger was so well equipped to do a job of hunting, or the desire to hunt, and consequent development of the equipment?" For Teilhard, radial energy always takes precedence. Consciousness causes development. Desire brings about somatic capability. Tigers lusted after deer before they became such efficient hunters of them.

So it will be in the future evolution of man. Evidence of a desire to share consciousness is already evident in the reliance we place in computers even today. This desire will, perhaps only after millenia, eventually bring about the development of the psychic and somatic organs to achieve the goal of shared consciousness.

If science today has had a positive effect on theology by forcing it to focus on the experiential, on the relational and processive, it might have had what some would perceive as a negative one in challenging the common understanding of the traditional proofs for the existence of God. Science seems to be on the side of those philosophers who maintain that our intellect serves us in conceiving the existent, not in establishing the existence of what is conceived. Only experience can establish existence.

Five forms of the argument for the existence of God are clearly enunciated by St. Thomas Aquinas. The first argument is from the need to have an unmoved mover. Nothing in our experience moves or changes itself, but movement is effected from without. To explain motion, then, either one must postulate an infinite chain of movers, each one moving another down the line, or else one must arrive somewhere in the chain at a mover who is himself unmoved, and that is God. Now philosophers say that it is not possible to have an infinite number of created realities. So there must be a God.

The second argument proceeds in a similar fashion. It examines causality. Nothing in our experience can be a cause of itself, but is caused by something without. If we experience effects, then either we must trace them back through an infinite chain of positive causes, or else somewhere in the chain arrive at a cause which is itself uncaused, and that is God.

The third argument postulates the necessity of an absolute, of a non-contingent reality to account for contingent being. Really this argument is the central one; all others flow from it. It proceeds this way. Nothing that we know in the universe necessarily exists. But one must account for existence. It can be accounted for only if we postulate a being that is absolutely necessary, a being that necessarily exists and is the reason in the ultimate analysis for the existence of contingent reality. That being is God.

The fourth argument is taken from the grades of perfection that we observe in all reality in the realm of our experience. In that experience we ascertain that no single being represents the absolute perfection of what it is. The multiplicity of beings does manifest a certain unity of the class or order in which they exist, since they all are to some extent alike. They all evidence a participation in the absolute perfection possible for that order. But none of them is absolutely perfect. The absolute perfection of the order has to exist outside of the order itself. And that is God.

The final argument reveals God as the supreme intelligence. Purposefulness always discloses intelligence. When we find purposefulness in creation, we know that there was an intelligence behind it. And the intricacy, multiplicity and clarity of purposefulness in the universe shows forth a supreme intelligence — God's.

Everyone can see how heavily these proofs rely on the principle of causality. Yet this principle is challenged from almost every quarter of scientific research today. The scientist shies away from explaining the connection between what we ordinarily call cause and effect by means of some law of necessity or inner cogency, and seeks an explanation, as we have said, in appealing to statistics. While the universe may be radically random in its operation, in the case of certain connections the outcome is predictable. And the prediction will be right in a very large number of cases. But not necessarily in absolutely every case.

Let us take an example. Suppose I want to walk through a door the way Jesus is reported to have done after his resurrection. I really cannot count on doing it. And some people would say that it's absolutely impossible. But, on the other hand, I know that both my body and the wall are composed of atoms. My atomic mythology tells me that there may be some solid particles, a nucleus and lighter planetary electrons in atoms but they are infinitesimally small. They are surrounded by very (comparatively speaking) large areas of empty space. Both my body and the wall I want to pass through are composed mostly of empty space. So the wall should offer little or no resistance to my passage? Wrong! There are force fields randomly arranged in both my body and the wall that prevent the passage I contemplate. There is an extremely high probability (enough to say that the wall is a cause of my inability to do what I want) that I will not be able to penetrate the wall even in thousands and thousands of attempts. The energy fields in both my body and the wall are arranged too much at random almost all of the time to prevent my doing what I want. The atomic forces in the wall will oppose and offer great resistance to the forces in my body unless they are perfectly arranged and phased. I can try and try again and again and I will always fail until I conclude that the wall is the reason or cause that I cannot do what I want. But is it possible, say, several times in a googolplex of tries, that the forces in both my body and the wall will be so arranged and phased so that they will not oppose penetration?

Science says "Yes!" Philosophers may say "No, because there is a universal and absolute law of causality." But in today's world, science is believed. The law we call the principle of causality is only a rule of thumb; it has a very high degree of statistical probability in its favor. A couple of times in a googolplex of tries it might not work. So there is no inner necessity in the law of causality, and the arguments for the existence of God remain under challenge by science.

A second problem that modern science raises for the traditional proofs for the existence of God arises from the notion that all reality must fall into one or other category of a binary state or condition. It must be either on or off. Nothing else is possible. The fact is that we find and experience the universe in the "on" position. It is there. Why can we not say that it was always on? Why do we have to suppose that at one time it was "off" and consequently needed someone or something to turn it

on? Do we not project upon the universe our own
subjective experience? Indeed we are well aware of
the fact that there was once a time when we were
off; something or someone turned us on. But why
do we project our history upon the universe? To the
scientist it seems to be done gratuitously. True, the
universe has undergone many vicissitudes. It may
have passed through many stages of development
and may be headed for many more. But the basic
stuff out of which it is made is presumed to have
been always here. There is no good reason for
saying that at one time it was not.

The theologian has tried to counter these challenges by adducing some new perspectives. Some
theologians offer a new argument for the existence
of God from the intelligibility of the universe, a
given, they say, of philosophy and theology. If the
universe were not intelligible, science would be
operating in vain. The scientist would be only playing games. This new argument sees God not merely
as being itself, *ipsum esse,* but *ipsum esse intelli-
gere,* the ultimate in intelligence and intelligibility.
It proceeds like this: if the real is completely intelligible, then God exists; but the real is completely
intelligible; therefore God exists.

Then again the objections of science have produced a refined and possibly more correct understanding of the traditional arguments of St.
Thomas Aquinas for the existence of God. Basically,
all of the arguments are in one way or another
reducible to the third way, the argument from the
contingency of the reality that we experience. This

seems to be the key argument. Our observation of the mechanisms of the cosmos indicate that it is not capable of producing, only becoming. We cannot prove that it has ever created being from nothing. The cosmos seems to be able only to redistribute and change the form of the various existents or beings that compose it, never to give rise to being or existence itself. The argument from contingency states that whatever can actually be in a condition or state other than we find it in, other than it is, is capable of not being at all. Therefore something has to account for its being — God. Thus while the law of causality operating in relation to the various components of the universe can be challenged and reduced to an issue of statistical probability, the law of causality as applied to being itself must remain intact. God and God alone can account for being.

Through these arguments the challenge of science can be evaded by an escape to an area of human consciousness that does not properly deal with the object of science, with the empirical. The theologian can elude the scientific blockade by fleeing to the metaphysical. But can the scientist, who certainly can claim that human thought processes lie within the realm of the empirical, then apply the rule of statistical probability to them, and assert that there is no inner necessity in logical arguments either? It may well be that the tug of war between science and theology in the question of the existence of God is destined to go on for some time.

One of my favorite Scripture passages is the little

story that is told in the Book of Exodus [33/18-23].
Here Moses expresses a hope that I believe is entertained by many people today. Moses asks God to
manifest himself to him. Moses desires to see
Yahweh as he really is, and thus dispel any doubts
about his existence. But of course both he and
Yahweh know the rule that Scripture sets forth. No
one can see the face of Yahweh and live. But
Yahweh, because Moses is his special friend, offers
to make a concession. He tells Moses that he must
stand on a rock and place himself in a cleft between
two rugged mountains. Thus he will be properly
braced for the vision that will be granted to him.
Yahweh tells Moses that he will hold his hand over
Moses' eyes so that for a while he will see nothing.
But when he takes his hand away, Moses will have a
fleeting glimpse of the back side of Yahweh himself!

Even today the rule set down in Scripture must
prevail. No one can see the face of God and live.
But the challenge of science has focussed the attention of theologians upon God today in a way that is
unprecedented in history. The scientific study of
both man and the rest of creation has enabled us
today to see, indeed, very much more than just the
back side of the Lord!

Chapter IV

CREATION

THE theological doctrine of creation implies the total production of a reality in its very being itself. Creation means that there can be no pre-existent reality out of which another is made. In a looser, non-technical sense the word "creation" is sometimes applied to the production of something out of pre-existent materials, but one which involves quite a bit of ingenuity or artistic skill. In this sense an Easter bonnet can be a creation. But when the word is used in the technical, theological sense it implies a power that is exclusively God's. For an infinite power is required to bridge the gap between the non-existent and the existent. Traditionally, in Christian circles creation is considered to be a free choice of God. God did not have to create anything: creation is the result of a divine decision. Many theologians teach that time began to exist simultaneously with creation; creation and time are inextricably linked. Christian theology has also called attention to the vestiges of God that are to be found in creation. Just as any manufactured object betrays some of the characteristics and qualities — especially the intelligence — of its maker, so too the universe itself reveals in some measure the awesome power and supreme intelligence of its creator. Creation is an act of God that occurred once-for-all.

God's follow-up on creation has been designated in different terms. The sustaining of created reality in being is called conservation; God's cooperation with the activity of the on-going processes of the universe is termed concurrence; and the direction and guidance of all created beings to the goal that God has set for them is called providence.

The story of creation which has influenced Jewish as well as Christian thought is the one that is contained in the first chapters of the Book of Genesis in the Bible. Initially this story was taken quite literally by theologians as well as by the populace at large. The first element of the story to be eroded was the idea of the days of creation. There was a time when the word "day" was considered literally to be a period of 24 hours. It was gradually expanded into years, into centuries, into thousands upon thousands of years, and finally into immeasurably long eons of time as evolutionary theory began to make its presence felt. After this, other elements of the story began to be taken in a more metaphorical sense, until today, in many quarters, the whole story is viewed as strictly mythological.

We must emphasize again, however, that by myth we mean the objectification in our world of a reality that takes place in another world of which we cannot be directly conscious. The creative act, after all, has to be, as we said, an action of God, and in this world we can have no direct consciousness of God and his activity.

Since it is the result of God's direct activity,

created being in itself, as it emanated from the hand of God, must be considered as good, and in no way evil. The Church has always understood that the refrain continuously repeated in the creation epic in the Bible, namely, that God saw that all he created was good, is a part of the myth that is meant to be taken literally. The Roman Catholic Church has defined in its councils that whatever God created is good as it issues from the creative act. Whatever man perceives as evil in creation has become evil due to its own activity and apart from the intention of God. This does not mean that God created the best possible universe. Roman Catholic theology has always acknowledged the presence in creation of what has been called "metaphysical evil," that is the lack of further possible perfection. From the human standpoint a better job could have been done on the universe. But this is the system that best suits God's purposes.

The lack of further perfection in the universe leads to the consideration of one of the most difficult pastoral problems that has to be handled by the rabbi, minister or priest. It is the question of the experience of physical evil in the life of human beings. The existence of moral evil, sin, does not present such a difficulty. Most people understand that if God was to have a free universe, that is, if the pinnacle of his creation, man, was to be like him, and enjoy a perfect freedom of choice, sin had to become a possibility. The real problem exists only in respect to physical evil. When people witness the death of a beloved one, when they are afflicted

with serious disease, when they experience the loss
of all their possessions or their security, they are
bound to ask the question: "Why? How can this be
if there is a God who is good?" This question has
been continuously on the lips of suffering mankind, and Christian theology has considered it in
the light of a number of theories that are grounded
in revelation, in the Bible itself.

The first theory traces the origin of physical evil
to moral evil. Because man sinned, evil came into
his world. Yet man had to be capable of sinning;
otherwise he would not have a will that would be
perfectly free. Give man a free will and you give
him the possibility of inflicting evil upon others.
Yet it is in free choice that there is also the unre-
stricted potential to love and, in choosing to love,
human beings become, in the most perfect way
imaginable, images of God. This is precisely what
God intended when he created mankind.

In many places Scripture places the reason for
suffering, for physical evils of all kinds, and for
death itself, in the fact of man's sinfulness. Clearly
this is the position of the friends of Job when they
confront the problem of his suffering. They tell
him that he must acknowledge his sin, that certainly he must have sinned otherwise God would
not have afflicted him the way he did, and that he is
living a lie in continuing to protest his innocence in
the face of his suffering. It would be a cruel and
unjust God who would punish those who have not
offended him. To continue to protest one's innocence when confronted with suffering has in itself

to be sinful. It would presume that God is punishing one who is innocent — and that is absolutely unthinkable. Yet through all of this Job knows that he has not sinned. Job is wiser than his friends. He is aware, because of his experiences, of the fact that sinfulness is not the only reason why man is subject to suffering and physical evil of all kinds. There have to be other reasons.

But the idea that physical evils are traceable to sin is also found in many other places in Scripture. When Joshua is defeated in battle, he immediately suspects that someone in his company has sinned, and discovers that Achan has violated the command of Yahweh and taken booty in battle. Sometimes a whole people has to suffer because of the sin of one man. Thus Joshua asks [22/20]: "When Achan, son of Zerah, betrayed his trust in regard to the ban, did not the wrath of the Lord come down upon the whole community of Israel, although he was only one man?" If we accept this principle we also see why, for instance, all Israel was threatened with punishment because of the sin of David. And we also see why popes like Innocent III and Boniface VIII could place whole nations under the ban of interdict because of the waywardness of their kings. They justified their action by an appeal to Scripture.

Another familiar case: the sailors on the ship that gave Jonah passage were convinced that the terrible storm they were experiencing was due to the wrath of some god vented against one of their passengers. Whey they confronted him with this issue, Jonah

came forward and acknowledged that he was fleeing from his God, that he had refused to accept the
task that was given to him by his God, and so that
he might well be responsible for the fury of the
storm. Immediately he was cast overboard, and the
story tells us that the storm then subsided, and the
ship presumably was saved.

The idea that physical evil began with the sin of
Adam is one that has dominated Christian theology
for many centuries. Had Adam not sinned, we
would not have had to die. There would be no
sickness; there would be no deformities; there
would be no setbacks or problems for mankind.
Grace would have prevailed, and sin would have
been conquered. Our lower appetites would have
been perfectly subjected to reason. It would not be
necessary for us to study and labor to gain knowledge; like Adam and the angels we would have had
infused knowledge. We would also have been born
into the world as friends of God, as possessing his
gift of grace, basking in his love and so manifesting
him in the most perfect way possible in this world.
The world would have been a paradise always just
as it was initially.

Christian doctrine clearly asserts that Jesus had
to suffer the way he did because of the sinfulness of
the human race. Though Jesus himself was innocent of all sin, he took upon himself the burden of
the world's sinfulness. So he had to pay the penalty.
To imitate him sometimes even those who, like Job,
are innocent have to suffer. But always, in the case
of physical evil, sin is the culprit.

The second explanation for physical evil given in the Scriptures is that it is a corrective measure. Setbacks, suffering and death exist for man's own good. They purge man, humble him, make him aware of his own dependency upon God, and so are agents of wisdom which can strengthen and perfect man spiritually. Think of the mother who discovers her tiny child playing with a butcher knife in the kitchen. The child is enjoying himself immensely, but she must take the knife away from him, and by depriving him for a time of one liberty or another warn him that he must never do this again. What she does is for his own correction. It is ultimately for his own good that he suffers deprivation and a seeming lack of love. Indeed it is because she loves him so much that the mother treats her child in this way. There is also a hint from Scripture that when a person is visited with physical evils of one kind or another it is a sign of God's special love. Sometimes God tests people in this way in order to give them an opportunity to advance in love of him. So the experience of setbacks and suffering may well be an indicator of divine predilection. The Book of Proverbs proposes [3/11]: "Whom Yahweh loves, he rebukes, and he allows the son whom he loves to suffer." This theological position is also expressed with crystal clarity in the Book of Judith [8/25-27]: ". . . let us give thanks to the Lord our God who, as he tested our ancestors, is now testing us. Remember how he treated Abraham, all the ordeals of Isaac, all that happened to Jacob in Syrian Mesopotamia while he kept the sheep of Laban, his mother's brother. For as these ordeals were intended by him to search their hearts, so now this is not vengeance that God exacts against us, but a warning inflicted by the Lord on those who are near his heart.''

The third consideration of the problem of physical evil that is to be found in Scripture does not really attempt to give an answer or solution, or to assign a particular cause. You will remember how, at the end of the Book of Job, Yahweh himself appears to address the issue and provides his own reflection in the dispute between Job and his friends. From the heart of a whirlwind Yahweh gives not an answer, but proposes a question: Who can know the ways of the Lord? Job knows then that man cannot really understand or accept the reason for physical evil. The purpose that God has in mind lies buried deep in his heart. It is not for man to know. It is not even an issue to speculate on. Thus Job responds [42/1-3]: ''I know that you are all-powerful: what you conceive you can perform. I am the man who obscured your design with my foolish words. I have been addressing issues I cannot comprehend, marvels that are beyond me and my perception.'' The person who has faith in God and truly loves him must simply accept whatever suffering comes his way without trying to lay blame or assess reasons. His trust in God will prompt him to believe that God does have some purpose in mind and will eventually bring greater good out of suffering.

In our day, science has expended much effort in

investigating the question of the origin of the universe. The so-called "big bang" theory enjoys great popularity. According to it all the matter that we now find in the universe was concentrated initially in an extremely small space. In some kind of cataclysmic explosion that took place eons and eons ago it suddenly was propelled outward from this center to form what we now know as the expanding universe. Evidence for this theory is gathered from a study of the spectra of distant stars. In the diffraction of light from these stars we find significant changes occurring at the low frequency, or red end, of the spectrum: the so-called red shift. In accordance with the Doppler effect, which proposes that when objects are moving away from each other the lower frequency end of emitted radiation is affected, and conversely, when objects are moving toward each other the high frequency end manifests a change, since it is not the violet or high frequency end of the light spectrum which is affected, but the red or low frequency end, we must conclude that these stars and light emitting objects everywhere in the universe are moving away from some center.

But what about the concentration of matter in a relatively small space before the big bang? How did it arrive where it was and in the condition in which it was? Science has almost nothing to say about this. It is simply presumed that matter was there. The scientist does not have great difficulty in supposing that matter/energy in the universe is eternal. It always was and always will be, though because of entropy, its distribution is continuously affected. Some scientists believe that there might be evidence for an oscillatory condition of matter/energy in the universe. They opine that when the far-flung matter at the edge of the universe has gone out far enough, the outward movement will cease and an inward one will begin. The inception of this new phase will be signaled by a violet shift. The matter in the universe, they say, is like a rubber band. When it reaches the limits of expansion, it will again begin to contract. Some believe that this oscillatory motion has been going on forever and will continue forever. It takes billions and billions of years for the completion of each oscillatory phase, and just when the reversal will take place cannot at this time be predicted.

Scientists tell us that if the universe supports a sufficient amount of mass, this theory of a continuous oscillation would have plausibility. Opponents of the theory, in assaying the amount of mass, find that it falls short and project that the universe will continue to expand forever. Proponents of the theory feel that there is sufficient amount of mass to support it. Currently many think that the whole issue hinges upon the neutrino. It was previously believed that the neutrino is, strange as it may seem, a particle without any mass. Some more recent studies tend to support the idea that the neutrino might have an infinitesimal amount of mass. If this is true, the amount of mass in the universe will have to be recalculated, and it may well be that then scientists will conclude that it is sufficient to support the notion of a universe oscillating forever. After billions and billions of years the matter in the universe will again return to a very small area of concentration, and the big bang will happen all over again. The universe will once again have been recreated.

Other scientists, though their number seems to be growing smaller today, advance a theory of continuous creation of matter. From the widely diffused gases and larger particles that are encountered after a star has exploded or spent its life, through the influence of gravitational and other forces, new stars begin to be formed. It is a process that does not occur occasionally, but has been going on and will go on continuously in the universe. The universe is continuously dying and rising again. Entropised energy is somehow recouped and enables the process to continue *ad infinitum.* Thus it would seem, that while in this theory the universe itself is not viewed as oscillating, certain portions at least are. Matter first disintegrates, and then rebuilds itself again into complex forms.

Many theologians are telling us today that it is not the business of theology to describe the origin of the universe. They feel that the creation myth in the Bible, if understood correctly, conveys only one simple message. It really gives us no information whatsoever about the origin of the universe. It is meant to tell us about ourselves — to explain a facet of human life, a phenomenon of the human psyche that everyone experiences. Friedrich

Schleiermacher has made us aware that we all experience our creatureliness. We have a unique sense of dependence that is the source of all human religiosity. And many present-day theologians point to the creation myth as a most valuable symbol responding to this sense of dependence. Man needs to explore his roots beyond the point to which empirical science can take him. Driven by feelings of creatureliness the human being can never be satisfied until he learns about the Creator. The creation myth uncovers for man not only the secret of his own origin, but that of all the creatures that are his companions in his journey through space-time. The mythology of the creation epic transcends for man the mythology of empirical science.

Science generally does not concern itself with the problem of evil as such; that is a matter for philosophy and theology; but it does deal with the concrete, particular ills and difficulties that beset mankind. Indeed, as Teilhard de Chardin indicates, when one understands and appreciates the process nature of the universe there really can be no *problem* of evil. There is evil all right, but it should not create a problem for one who is familiar with the scientific view of the world. Teilhard points out that union always implies a loss. But it is absolutely necessary for continued gain. When the different particles of the universe complexify they have to lose their individuality: they have to shuck off the comfortable ways of their former state of existence.

It cannot be otherwise. But without complexification they remain just what they are; they do not ascend to newer and more significant states of being. As a theologian, Teilhard states that in creating a multiplicity of perfectible beings, God opened the way to the reality that people often perceive and take as evil. The process that is going on in the universe, necessary as it is, is the root of all evil.

Evil, according to Teilhard, is perceived by mankind in three different areas of the complexifying universe.

First, there is the evil of plurality. Beings will multiply and use up the limited resources that sustain them in such a way as to deprive similar beings of the possibility of survival. Yet a certain concentration of individuals in the same species is necessary, both for the survival of the species, and the possibility of developing better strains for the improvement of the stock. Yet when even space, *Lebensraum,* becomes a problem, some individuals are bound to experience deprivation.

The second evil is that of differentiation. The fact is, in our world, that different species can survive only by preying upon one another. Some of them have been adapted in an evolutionary process precisely to live off of others. The specificity of this dependence in some cases is shocking, and may be interpreted as a teleological challenge. In general, the principle of survival of the fittest seems established as one of the inexorable and seemingly cruel laws of nature. Yet differentiation also supplies the necessary challenge that each species needs to survive.

Arnold Toynbee tells a story about Scandanavian herring fishermen. Often they are out at sea for weeks at a time. The catch they have made and store in the great holds of the fishing vessels become more and more listless. By the time they reach port the fishermen are confronted with the problem of explaining to potential buyers why their catch seems to be on the verge of death, or at least looking very sick. One of the captains conceived the idea of putting a couple of barracudas in the tanks with the herring. Of course they ate a few. But even though the vessel was at sea for weeks when it reached port the catch was alert and looking alive. Buyers always sought out this vessel. Soon other fishermen were putting barracudas in their tanks too.

The example that Teilhard himself uses is very much to the point. He feels that the reason certain civilizations and cultures like the Polynesian did not become more progressive is that they were too isolated. The culture of the Mediterranean basin was as successful as it was because of the concentration of peoples of diverse ethnic and racial as well as cultural and religious backgrounds. So differentiation provides an atmosphere actually of growth for both the refinement of the species in the present and the emergence of higher and better adapted forms in the future.

Finally, there is the evil of metamorphosis which

makes us aware of the fact that often, in order to attain a fuller and more perfect situation of existence, it is necessary to shuck off older and less useful adaptations — although indeed these seem more comfortable and safe. Change is always difficult. There is always risk and uncertainty when one departs from tried and true ways. Yet progress depends upon the ability to take such a risk. Whatever impedes or impairs beneficial transformation must be discarded. In our system, with its very limited resources, there cannot be any gain without some loss. It is necessary to let loose of what one has become used to, what often is perceived as a source of security and hard-won peace in order to pass on to higher and better things.

For modern science the universe is continuously in process. But one can hardly envision a process situation where these three types of evil would not be encountered. The philosopher and the theologian must always appreciate the fact that evil is a relative thing. What is looked upon as evil for one being may well insure the survival and well being of another. When the lion in the Serengeti Plain attacks the wildebeest, it is bad for the wildebeest, but good for the lion. It is not easy to think of any type of physical evil that does not bring about some good for some being. Even sickness and death clears the earth and makes room for future generations. Physical evil seems always to have an aspect of good relative to some other reality in the universe. There does not seem to be any that is just bad. This is what science can make us aware of.

And this outlook on creation can assist the theologian and his clientele, the pastoral community, better to appreciate the nature and significance of physical evil. It makes it easier to see how God can and always does bring good out of evil.

Theology and science alike have manifested a good deal of interest in the origins of mankind. Traditionally, theology has followed very closely the biblical story of the creation of man. For it, Adam was an individual, the first man. He was composed, as all men are, of body and soul. Man's body was produced directly by God from inanimate matter. His soul was the very breath of God. To be sure it was not considered as some kind of divine emanation, but it, too, was directly created by God from nothing. Adam's companion, the woman Eve, was also directly created by God. Her body was taken by God from the body of Adam; her soul was created from nothing just as Adam's was. The whole race of man was derived from this first couple, Adam and Eve. And since Eve was herself taken from Adam's body, mankind in its totality was considered to be descended from the first man, Adam.

The first two humans, Adam and Eve, were endowed with special supernatural gifts, that is, gifts which are over and above what belongs to human nature constitutively, consecutively or exigetively. The most precious of these supernatural gifts was substantially supernatural; that is, under no circumstance in any way could nature be considered as connected with this gift. True, it complemented man's natural endowment, but it carried him so far beyond his natural situation as to bring him into a totally different arena of action, that of divine love. It was the gift of grace, the gift of an intimate friendship with God himself, whereby man could no longer be considered just a creature of God like the rest, but had now to be regarded as a member, as it were, of God's own family, one capable of the same kind of love that characterizes the very essence of God himself. Then, too, primitive man enjoyed the modally supernatural gifts. These were ones that under different times and circumstances might have been associated with natural developments, but which in the way or at the time they were received could not have been produced by nature. The modally supernatural gifts which traditional theology attributes to primitive man are those of immortality, which insured man's immunity from having to die; integrity, by which the lower appetites were subjected to reason; and infused knowledge which eliminated the necessity of having to study in order to learn. All these were the marvelous adornment of the first human couple.

Today we know that the biblical description of the creation of the first man has been derived simply by reversing what is observed as occurring at and after death. In a relatively dry, desert-like atmosphere, bodies eventually wind up as a kind of dust. What, however, one first observes when a person dies is that he no longer breathes. At this juncture the body remains pretty well as it was in life;

but breathing has ceased. The person is no longer
considered to be alive. Eventually the body disintegrates and is dissolved into a kind of powdery dust.
Given enough time, even the skeleton will disappear. So the story of the creation of Adam was
concocted by a simple reversal of this process.

Hebrew thought definitely distinguishes the dead
from the living. And it also advocates the unity of
the human person. The breath of God that is in
man simply gives him life. The notion of the human
composite of body and soul is definitely Greek. The
body-soul dichotomy comes from Aristotle and not
from the Hebrew Bible. In accordance with the
Aristotelian notion of matter and form as the ultimate constituents of worldly reality, human beings
have been considered by theologians to be composed of body and soul, matter and spirit. The soul
is seen to be simple, that is, not having parts outside of parts, and unique for each individual.
Because it is spiritual, it is immortal: it cannot
disintegrate. It is the direct product of divine
creation not only in the case of Adam but also in
that of each and every of his descendants. It is the
seat of man's higher faculties. In it reside the
abilities of reasoning and choosing. As a spiritual
reality, man's soul is essentially independent of the
body; it can exist outside of the body. But as long
as it is in the body it depends upon bodily activities
(like those of the brain) for its functioning, that is,
for the use of intellect and will. The soul is not to be
located in any particular part of the body (Des-
cartes wanted to place it in the pineal gland) but the

whole and entire soul is in each and every part of the body as well as in the whole body itself.

The scientist traces the emergence of man from lower forms of life through an evolutionary process. The process was gradual, spanning millions and millions of years. At what precise time the human being actually emerged so that he was entirely distinguishable as such from other forms of life cannot be pinpointed in these eons of development. The body, the configuration and posture of which we were eventually to recognize as man's, developed very slowly from prehominid forms. Cephalic variation and growth highlighted the drift from the lower to the higher. But that brain which was ultimately to distinguish itself as the instrument of self-reflective consciousness developed at a painstakingly slow pace.

Much like the ancient Hebrews, scientists today regard man as an organic unity; they do not go along with the Greek dichotomy — there is no reason for dividing man into a material or bodily element on the one hand and an immaterial or spiritual one on the other. When a scientist is able to vary the circumstances or conditions under which a particular organ operates and note statistically verifiable variations in the behavior of the organ itself, he is apt to suspect that the organ itself is involved in the production of the results he has observed. The neurosurgeon notes drastic changes in the behavior of a person after a commissurotomy, or severing of the fibers of the *corpus callosum,* the connecting network of nerves between the two hemispheres of the brain. Drastic changes in perception occur. The person may be reading a book, but he will read only half a page vertically and act as if the result made sense to him. Everyone is familiar with the sometimes astounding personality changes that occur after a prefrontal lobotomy. Recent investigations have attempted to single out and correlate the activities associated with the left and right hemispheres of the human brain. Commissurotomized patients have helped immensely in this endeavor and, as research continues, more and more is being learned especially about conscious functions which seem to be the product of the less dominant side of the brain.

The scientist, then, tends to attribute the functions of man which many philosophers and theologians associate with his spiritual nature, with his soul, to the functioning of neuronal tissue within the brain.

This is not to say that the scientist today is fully satisfied that he has discovered the seat of and full explanation for the phenomenon of consciousness itself. Even for the scientist consciousness remains somewhat of a deep mystery. There is no doubt that it is associated with neuronal functioning. Yet it does not seem that consciousness, in the sense in which we know and experience it, can be attributed just to a bundle of neurons. It seems much more complex than that. There is, however, a certain correlation that is possible. When cephalic neurons reach a certain mass and pattern certain effects we attribute to consciousness do occur. And when this mass becomes gigantic, as in the case of the human brain, even self-reflective conscious results are observable. But it is all a very delicate process, and even such seemingly minor interferences as a slight concussion or certain chemicals can interrupt the steady flow of consciousness. In the case of consciousness the whole does seem to be greater than the mere sum of its parts. Thus many scientists do leave open the possibility of accounting for many of the phenomena of man's higher life only through the agency of some kind of spirit or soul that must be an integral part of the human makeup. Since this immaterial element would not fall under the scope of his empirical investigation, however, the scientist would leave it to the philosopher or the theologian to speculate about its precise nature and function.

Would it not be wonderful if the Church would take science as its mentor at least in regard to one thing? As we said, science makes pronouncements that are only temporary and provisional, not final and absolute. But unfortunately the Church has never appreciated the value of this approach. Consequently it has had to make what seem to its adherents embarrassing (although the official Church does not seem to be the least bit abashed by this fact) retrenchments of one kind or another. Although there has not been to this date any official acknowledgement of error on the part of the official Church in the case of Galileo Galilei, documents do presume a Copernican rather than a Ptolomeic solar system. But at least at the grass-roots level the rapid advance of evolutionary ideas from the status of hypothesis, through that of theory, to one of fairly well established fact has forced even the official Church to modify somewhat its initial thinking about the origins of mankind.

Of course some sectors of the Church even today, despite all scientific progress, still sustain a literal interpretation of the events described by Genesis. We all know of the recent law suits in a number of states which have concerned themselves with the demand for equal time for the teaching of creationism with that of evolutionary theory in public schools. While generally these suits have been resolved on the basis of the principle of separation of Church and state, the fact that a fairly large number of people support the equal time proposition shows that even today there remains in some quarters massive resistance to scientifically established data. In the Roman Catholic Church, usually quite conservative of its dogmatic positions, some minimum progress has indeed been made.

On August 12, 1950 Pope Pius XII issued a memorable encyclical letter entitled *Humani generis*. The purpose of this document was to deal with some false opinions which threatened to undermine the foundations of Catholic doctrine. The pope asserted that some truths that have to do with God and man completely surpass the sensible order and demand self-surrender in faith and self-abnegation that they might bear fruit in practical life. He stated that the human intellect, in trying to deal with such truths, is hampered both by the activities of the senses and imagination and by evil passions that arise from original sin. He seemed to be appalled that some people, as he said, imprudently and indiscreetly hold that evolution, which, he maintains, has not been fully proven even in the domain of the natural sciences, explains the origin of all things, and that these persons audaciously support a monistic and pantheistic viewpoint that the world is in continual evolution. He pointed out how the Communists gladly subscribe to this opinion because they see it as antagonistic to the idea that there is a personal God, and welcome it as helping and aiding their own philosophy of dialectical materialism. He scorns those who would try to reduce to a minimum the meaning of certain Christian dogmas. He warns against changing the terminology that has been associated with these doctrines in the hope of making them more intelligible to a modern audience. The encyclical raps those who desire to depart from the literal meaning and interpretation of holy Scripture. He especially calls to task those theologians who would want to redefine the notion of the supernatural. He is greatly concerned over the fact that some theologians have parted ways with the idea of original sin proposed in the Council of Trent. He is taken aback by those who would question whether angels are personal beings, and whether matter and spirit differ essentially. He extols the traditional Scholastic philosophy because in his opinion it is

the only vehicle through which the teachings of the
Church can be rightly conveyed and appreciated.

The last part of the encyclical handles the question of the evolution of the human body in a more
specific way. The pope indicates that it would be
permissible for persons who are well experienced
both in the area of the human sciences and that of
sacred theology to enter into a dialogue and discussion on the issue of evolution, but only to the
extent that such interaction would deal with the
possibility of the human body originating from pre-
existent living matter rather than from a non-living
source. He indicates that the Catholic faith obliges
one to believe that souls are immediately created by
God. He warns that some have already rashly trans-
gressed this freedom of discussion which the
Church allows by acting as if the origin of the
human body from other living creatures were
already a certain and proven fact. He indicates that
revelation as preserved in tradition demands that
one exercise the greatest moderation and caution in
treating of this question, and that one ought not to
regard what seems only a hypothesis or at most a
theory as proven fact.

While there might be freedom of discussion on
this particular matter, he warns that no such liberty
exists in the case of another opinion, namely that of
polygenism. One may not hold that the human race
is derived from several different stocks, that there
might have been several pairs of first parents. It is
not permitted for the faithful to embrace any
opinion that would claim that either after Adam

there existed on earth true men who did not take their origin through natural generation from him as from a first parent, or that the word "Adam" could represent a number of first parents. He feels that such an assumption would call into question the traditional teaching of the Church in regard to original sin. It would threaten the dogmatic pronouncements of the councils, particularly the Council of Trent.

It should be pointed out that in many of his allocutions and pronouncements, especially toward the end of his life, Pius XII dealt with ethical issues which depended for their solution in large part upon obtaining accurate scientific data. In considering some of these publications, few would doubt that his scientific advisers, even for their time, were not always well informed. This is exemplified, for instance, in an address that Pius XII gave to geneticists on September 7, 1953 [*"Soyez les bienvenus" Acta Apostolicae Sedis* 45/596-607]. In this address he seems to indicate that genetic manipulation is not possible. Indeed, acquired traits do not affect genetic tissue. Any modifications made in the genes are not on a reliable or predictable basis communicated to descendants [p. 598]. Yet even at that time, experiments with, for instance, fruit flies, had reliably introduced a number of transmitted characteristics like color, shape of wings, etc., to the extent of producing in the laboratory a new biological species.

But even at the time the papal encyclical *Humani generis* was issued monogenetic evolution, which

was the only form it permitted, was not widely sustained in scientific circles. Certainly in the later development of evolutionary theory polygenism was
simply presupposed as a norm for the consideration
of the origins of humankind. Shortly after the
publication of this encyclical the theologian who
wanted to accept evolutionary theory would not
find himself in accord with the views of scientists
were he to advance the idea of a monogenetic evolutionary process. To be true to the science of his
time he had to find a way of squaring polygenism
with theology. Since the principal obstacle in his
way was the conciliar doctrine regarding the nature
of original sin — actually the position taken by
Pius XII in his encyclical was one which in his eyes
was necessitated by the pronouncements of the
Council of Trent on original sin — the key to the
solution of the problem had to be sought in a reap-
praisal of the doctrine of original sin. Only by re-
assessing the significance of this doctrine and exploring the possibility of a new understanding of
it could the theologian establish a much desired interface between the scientific doctrine of evolution
and the dogmas of his religion.

Chapter V

ORIGINAL SIN

THE Reformers taught that original sin severely impaired human functioning. Because of it, without the help of God's grace, man simply cannot avoid sinning. He is not able to choose the good. He is doomed always to commit sin. He has no freedom of election. Only the grace of God can save him, can set him free so that he can choose the good. For John Calvin the grace of God is irresistible. With grace man is not only free to choose the good, he *must* choose the good.

The Roman Catholic doctrine elaborated by the Council of Trent rejects these ideas. The human will remains free even in this present sinful condition. Even without grace man is capable of accomplishing some good. When one considers individual incidents or cases, any person who is normal is able to choose either good or evil without any help from outside. Original sin may weaken freedom, but it does not rob one of it. It is true that man cannot indefinitely avoid sin in this present condition by sheer will power. Both as regards his body and his soul man is worse off in his present state than he would have been had he not sinned. In the long run he does need God's grace in order to live a good and decent life. Even though in each individual case he could choose good over evil without grace, he does need grace to mount a whole series of good acts. He could never lay claim to heaven without grace. Grace is needed for salvation, but not for each and every good action.

What then precisely is original sin as it is understood in Roman Catholic theology? Most theologians look upon it simply as a deprivation of grace. Because of the sin of his ancestors, man comes into this world without enjoying God's friendship, his grace. Yet grace is necessary for man to attain the goal or end that God has established for him. Man ultimately needs grace, then, in order to observe the law in a substantial as well as a salutary way, even though in each individual case when a person is confronted by a precept of the law, substantial observance of it is possible even without grace.

Four main points of doctrine concerning original sin are set down by the Council of Trent. Original sin comes down to us by natural generation from Adam who is the head of the race. Adam held in trust for all of his descendants the supernatural gifts with which humanity was initially endowed. Had he not sinned, all would have received them from the first moment of their existence. But as it is, through his sin, he lost them, and so all are born into this world in a deprived condition. The Council insists on natural generation as the vehicle by which this sin is transmitted; it is not due to concupiscence or communicated by bad example as some have taught. Thus Jesus did not incur the debt of original sin since he was not naturally generated. He was not conceived in a natural way from Mary and Joseph, but through the special action of the Holy Spirit.

Secondly, the Council teaches that this sin personally affects every member of the race. The dogma of the Immaculate Conception of the Virgin Mary, defined some years later, exempted the mother of Jesus, because of her special relationship to him, from the debt of incurring original sin. The unity and solidarity of the race in sin is considered to be an important part of this dogma. Jesus and Mary alone stand outside of what Augustine called the *massa damnata*, the condemned lot of mankind.

Thirdly the Council asserts that human beings are worse off both in body and soul because of original sin. Though they are not at all deprived of what would be coming to them naturally, they experience the rebellion of lower appetites against reason. The functioning of both intellect and will is impaired. Traditionally, the catechism has expressed it this way: because of original sin our intellects are darkened and our wills are weakened so that we become more prone to committing personal sin.

Fourthly, Jesus by his expiatory sacrifice restored the possibility of intimate friendship with God; that is, he won back for man the grace that was lost through original sin. Of course, the modally supernatural gifts of immortality, integrity and infused knowledge were not restored, but the really essential one was. So Jesus becomes a new Adam; he founds a new race of men, men who are once again friends of God. Just as the first Adam lost grace for all of his followers, so Jesus restores it to all of his. There is possible for man, because of Jesus, a new unity and new solidarity in grace and love.

Of course Christian churches of many varieties link the doctrine of original sin to that of the necessity of baptism. We can be incorporated into the new race, that founded by Jesus, only through this sacrament of initiation. All human beings stand in need of redemption, since they are born in sin. So even infants must be baptized. Though they themselves cannot put forth that act of faith, that act of adherence to Christ the new Adam, that is necessary to escape the toils of original sin, the Church, through their sponsors, pledges for them what they are unable to do. Baptism, as we have seen, symbolizes their identity with Christ in his paschal mystery and consequently their incorporation into his mystical body, into the unity and solidarity of faith and love that characterizes redeemed humanity.

Roman Catholic theologians have been unanimous in insisting upon the necessity of baptism for salvation. They emphasize that it is not merely because of a precept of God or of the Church that infants must be baptized; baptism is a necessary medium of salvation: it is as impossible to get to heaven without baptism as it is to get to the moon without a spaceship. Three forms of baptism are proposed: baptism with water, which is the normal form of the sacrament; baptism with blood, which implies martyrdom for the faith, and baptism of desire, which consists of acts of faith, sorrow for sin and love of God — or simply, an act of perfect love of God. This last form of baptism, up until very recently in the history of Roman Catholic theology, was not considered possible for the infant. The only possible avenue of salvation for an infant was baptism with water, the formal sacrament, or with blood, like the infants which the Gospel says were massacred by King Herod in his attempt to do away with Jesus.

According to the teaching of the Council of Trent original sin is one that we have inherited, not committed. Yet sin must always be the result of man's free choice. Of course, theologians say, original sin, too, was the result of a free choice — albeit not of the person who bears its guilt — but of Adam who held in trust for humanity all the gifts of salvation. This situation is often compared to the case where the head of a household is given a large sum of money. If he uses the gift wisely and preserves it, the whole family and all his descendants benefit from it. But on the other hand, if he squanders it, it is their loss as well as his. The loss was due to a free choice, not of each and every member of the family, but of the head of the household who elected to act in the way he did. Only by another dole, by another free bestowal of an additional amount of money can they once again enjoy the benefits originally intended.

With today's views on the nature of the sacraments differing not a little from traditional ones,

Roman Catholic theologians are faced with the task of explaining just how the sacrament of baptism works *ex opere operato* — confers grace automatically, especially in the case of an infant. Some would say that if sin could be incurred without the cooperation of the infant, grace could be bestowed too. The older theology sees a kind of inpouring of grace into the human soul. Although the soul of an infant is incapable of human action, it must lie open, like all created reality, to divine activity. God as it were, bathes the infant in his love, and this brings about whatever response can be expected at this stage of the infant's development. But many modern theologians have come to regard the issue in a more concrete and practical way. They feel that all that one means by the *ex opere operato* effect of baptism is the guarantee of the Christian community to sequester that infant from the harmful effects of original sin. From the first moment of his dawning self-consciousness he will be protected and safeguarded from falling into sin by the prayers and guarantees offered by the whole community and by the guidance of his parents and sponsors in particular. The infant, from the moment of his baptism on, has the security of being a member of the Christian community, of being incorporated into Christ by the sacrament of initiation. The love of God is projected upon him in a very substantial way, in a very concrete and specific way through the care and concern of the Christian community.

In their view of original sin as well, many recent Roman Catholic theologians have moved away from more traditional understandings. Faced with the problem of polygenetic evolution — and the fact that monogenetic evolution is not seen as likely at all by today's scientists — they have thoroughly reviewed the Council of Trent's pronouncements on the whole issue of original sin. They have taken into account more the intent of the teaching than the actual wording. They regard the Council as being geared to assure the preservation of a number of traditional Roman Catholic dogmas against what were then considered to be the distortions of the Reformers. Chief among these dogmas has to be numbered the loss of the friendship of God, the loss of grace incurred by mankind as the result of some primitive fall. As was said, many theologians tend to place the very essence of original sin in this loss. All humans (Jesus and Mary excepted) are born into this world without grace, with their backs turned, as it were, on God. The primary effect of this situation or condition is an inclination toward personal sinful action that all experience. Because they are sinners, they have a proclivity toward further sinning. Sin begets sin.

If this is the essential dogma proposed by the Council of Trent, need there any longer be an insistence upon the idea that all human beings descended from a single couple? It would seem that just the fact of being human, of having taken origin from whatever human beings existed initially, is sufficient to establish the common state of sinfulness upon which the dogma dwells. Indeed, is there anyone contemplating the whole history of mankind as well as the present condition of crime in our society who would deny man's proclivity to evil?

Theologians in our time have arrived at a new understanding of original sin which avoids biological problems. It is the idea of *Weltsünde,* sin of the world. This new conceptualization emphasizes that original sin must be considered in the light of this single fact: that the world into which every human being is born has been deeply affected by the sins perpetrated by the original human beings, be they a single pair, or a whole group, or even several races. The fact is that all of them turned away from God and lost his gift of friendship. As a result an atmosphere of sin pervaded the world. As human beings are born into the world they breathe in this atmosphere. The world is like an aquarium that has been poisoned. No fish could escape unless it would be specially protected. From the very moment new fish are hatched they are affected by the poison. So it is with humanity. There is no escape from the power of sin that rules the world. Only the grace of Jesus Christ can guarantee immunity.

Proponents of this modern view of original sin insist that every human infant is pre-personally conditioned to commit sin. In other words, before a child comes to know the difference between good and evil he or she is already situated in a world that is infected with sin, and this condition has already predisposed the child to sin. But it is not by imitation of or following the example of his elders that the child is inclined to sin. The child does not just learn how to sin. It is because of the child's situation in a sinful world that sin already has a hold even before the child comes to recognize it for what it is.

The renowned Catholic theologian Karl Rahner takes a slightly different tack in redefining original sin. He proposes that despite polygenism there is always a basic unity and solidarity in the human race. This solidarity was initially assured by mankind's unitary supernatural orientation to Christ. The call to be one in Christ extended to every human forms much more of a bond among men than just physical descent from a common head, Adam. The radical inability in man's present state to respond to this call constitutes the very essence of original sin. Only through the grace of Christ is it possible to make a fitting response.

Great numbers of theologians today are following the lead of Rahner and claiming that the solidarity of the human race does not at all depend upon physical descent from common stock, but upon psychological, moral or other connections. Many stress the psychological unity of mankind such as is evident in the ability that people have to communicate with one another even though they speak different languages, and emanate from decisively different cultures. Whoever committed the first sin, whether it was a single individual or a whole group, started a chain reaction. The entrance of sin into the world precluded a God-intended human development which can now take place only with the help of the grace of Christ. So there is in the world a universal experience of guilt resulting

from this initial deviation from the call of God to
perfect unity and solidarity in his love.

Another group of theologians would identify
original sin with the ongoing process of sin in the
world. The proud structures that man has erected
for himself contain the roots of sinfulness. Here
one encounters such phenomena as institutional
racism, exploitation of the weak and poor and
political strangleholds that only violent revolution
can break. Liberation theologians see that the
Gospel message does contain what is necessary to
free mankind from servitude to these structures
that seem to have been erected precisely to allow
certain segments of society to abase and degrade
others. These structures are both the result of past
sinful action and the cause of continued sinful situations. In this theological perspective it would be
difficult to isolate original sin as a sin completely
distinct from personal sin. Really personal sin continually experienced and solidified in societal structures is the root-sin which theology interprets as
original sin. This has always been with mankind
from the time that human society began to exist,
and it will continue to dominate human life until
the Gospel message is fully accepted in faith and
God's grace prevails in society.

More in line with our purpose are those theological ideas that have in some way or other been derived from or otherwise connected with modern
scientific input has been very helpful in the current redefinition of original sin that is taking place
in theology. It seems a paradox that science, be-

cause of its evolutionary theory, is providing a challenge that forces a redefinition of original sin while at the same time it is providing clues as to how a challenge that forces a redefinition of original sin while at the same time is providing clues as to how a new definition might be elaborated. It remains only for the theologian to reassure the pastor and the believer at large that such a redefinition does not violate the tradition of the Church, and especially in the case of Roman Catholics, the teachings of the Council of Trent.

Pierre Grelot compares Paul's notion of original sin with the basic psychoanalytic theory of Sigmund Freud. Paul's obsession with the divided self, the disturbance over the war that he perceived being waged in his own members, his constant struggle to control himself, and his own admission that sometimes he does not really do what he wants to do are, in the opinion of Grelot, related to the conflictual elements in Freud's own theory of the composition of the human psyche — especially the notion of the conscious and unconscious self. The theological stance regarding an all-pervasive guilt condition (which original sin really is) fits in very well with Freud's oedipal complex. The idea of original sin as alienation from a Creator-Father is easily correlated with Freud's opinion relating to the origin of guilt in the dream of parricide. Just as the Christian connects personal sinfulness and guilt to the phenomenon of original sin, so the father of psychoanalysis traces psychic disturbances and problems to the oedipal complex. Neuroses and

psychoses have their origin in sexual rivalry and resulting warfare between father and son, mother
and daughter. The alienation of the psychotic or
neurotic person from society is comparable to the
alienation that sin also brings, an alienation from
God and from one's fellow-man.

Sharon MacIsaac also resorts to Freudian psychoanalytic theory in establishing an interface between theology and science on the matter of
original sin. She views original sin as both an
alienation from God and an inclination to evil
which is antecedent to any choice, and in this
proves herself to be quite traditional. Original sin is
for her a kind of pre-deliberative perversity. She
appeals to the teaching of St. Thomas Aquinas. She
points to the fact that Thomas recognizes as the
formal element in original sin this alienation from
God that has resulted from the loss of original
justice. She singles out concupiscence as the material element. The net result is a total disorientation
of the individual from God, his ultimate goal.

For Sigmund Freud a major consideration to be
dealt with in analyzing the source of human psychological problems is the dualism that he observed
as a characteristic of the human psyche. Man
stands torn between the superego and the id. Not
only conscious influences but, more importantly,
those that flow imperceptibly from the unconscious
affect human behavior. The superego tells man
what he must do and punishes him with guilt if he
does not do it. The id, the seething pit of passion,
drives him to do what he does not want to do.

MacIsaac derives the theological idea of concupiscence from this Freudian notion. And concupiscence is a source of sin, like original sin itself. Concupiscence is the radical disorientation of the human person from the control of reason which impairs the ability of the individual to live in accordance with the law of God. Concupiscence is, in the words of St. Thomas, material original sin.

If Freud felt that the ego, poised as it is between the opposing drags of the superego and id, could never really be at peace with itself, MacIsaac similarly relegates the disorientation of sinfulness in human life to the inability of the human person to cope with the impulse of the will toward the good and righteous on the one hand, and the debasing thrust of concupiscence on the other. But this radical dualism is simply a given of human nature: it is just a part of our existence. As such, of course, it cannot formally constitute sinfulness but is only its material element; but through it there is revealed man's condition of alienation. Of himself man is not able to muster the help needed to alleviate this situation; he must rely on God and his gift of grace.

It is true that today the whole package of Freudian theory is not widely accepted, even among psychoanalysts. Many simply do not subscribe to the doctrine of psychic dualism, the oedipus complex and the pansexual fundaments of the system in accounting for the origin of psychoses and neuroses in human life. The farther time removes us from the pioneering efforts of the originator of the psychoanalytic method, the more we are able to appreciate his really marvelous psychological insights, but the more we have to question the validity of some of his theoretical presuppositions. If the theologian is to enjoy a more reliable and permanent scientific basis for his understanding of the doctrine of original sin, he must look into other areas of scientific research than that of Freudian theory.

To me the most promising of these is the field of genetics. In the ultimate analysis, original sin, like all sin, is a preference of self over God and neighbor. It is definite disregard for the great commandment of love. All sin must be defined, as the Gospel indicates, with reference to altruistic love. If my actions do not reveal a love of God above all else, and a love of my neighbor like that I have for myself, I sin. Through original sin I am predisposed to prefer myself to God and neighbor. Original sin is inborn selfishness; it is an egocentricity that has become part of the human genetic heritage itself. We must not, of course, think of it as an inherited disease: it is only a proclivity to behave in an egotistical manner; it is part of the natural self-preservative defensive mechanisms of the race resulting from situations that arose in the very early history of mankind and that are continued in the helpless condition in which the human infant finds himself at birth — a condition that in the human infant, unlike almost any other animal infant, is to last for a considerable period of his early life.

Recent genetic research has addressed the problem of how environmental factors influence behavior patterns that eventually become incorporated in the genetic code and influence the further development of the species. A good deal of evidence points to the automatic assimilation of certain physical traits relating to environmental conditions into the genetic package. Everyone is familiar with the fact that persons who live at extremely high elevations, like those of the Andes mountains in South America, have an unusual concentration of hemoglobin in their blood and develop a much larger lung capacity which is unmistakably evidenced in their barrel-like chests. This is not just an environmental adaptation of the individual, but a genetic phenomenon: when children are born to parents who have these characteristics but move to lower elevations, the children, too, have these features suited for living at high altitudes. But there is also evidence pointing to the fact that behavior patterns can be inherited. These also insure the survival of the species — in certain circumstances even moreso than mere organic adaptation. When, in their previous history, certain species of animals learn how to cope with their environment and when these responses become automatic, it seems that eventually they influence the genetic code in such a way as to be able to be transmitted to the offspring of these species. This phenomenon is clearer in the behavior of lower animals than in that of higher, for it seems that the higher the animal is on the evolutionary scale, the more infants have to depend on learning behavior from their parents, and less is automatically transmitted in inborn responses through the genetic package. But even in the higher animals some traits are received, especially the most basic ones.

Laboratory evidence supports the conclusion that some behavioral traits stored in the nervous tissue of individuals can eventually work their way into the genes and produce the same recognizable patterns in the offspring.

Picture a laboratory room with four bare walls painted white, a plain floor, in the middle of which there is situated an incubator and a nest with four duck eggs, and a ceiling painted white with a single bare light bulb and a trolley wire. There is a one-way-mirror viewing point in one of the walls through which we can watch what happens as, one by one, the duck eggs hatch. The ducklings peck away, crack the shells and emerge, fluffing their feathers and preparing themselves for life in the outer world. Now across the trolley on the ceiling of the room an experimenter pulls a cardboard silhouette representing a local dove in flight, so that the shadow of the dove falls upon the newly hatched ducklings in their nest. We observe their behavior. It is as if nothing at all happened. The passage of the dove does not evoke any response at all in the ducklings. Next the experimenter pulls across the wire trolley the silhouette of a European duck hawk so that its shadow falls upon the nest of the hatchlings. Once again there is no sign of recognition. The ducklings continue their task of preening and exploring. But when the experimenter uses the silhouette of an indigneous duck hawk panic ensues. The ducklings scamper about, flopping outside the nest and seeking a hiding place. But there is no place to conceal themselves. Their frenetic behavior continues until the silhouette is drawn into a slot on the other side of the room. Then they regain their composure, and begin to resume routine tasks.

How did the newly hatched ducklings know the difference among the silhouettes of the various birds that were drawn across the ceiling? How could these infants, who have had no experience before of American, much less European duck hawks, recognize the one which might well have been a threat to their lives? They were sequestered from their mother who might have taught them or signalled them by her behavior that this was the particular species of bird that they must fear, that whenever they encountered this species of bird flight was in order. The only logical conclusion we can draw is that recognition of the enemy and the proper reaction to his presence was inborn. It had to be part of the ducklings' genetic heritage. Perhaps in the long history of ducks on this continent those who responded to an encounter with a duck hawk by flight and hiding survived, while those who did not perished. Either there was something already in their genes that made those who escaped behave in the salvific way they did, or else the fact that flight in this instance was salvific became in some coded way imprinted on their

genes, so that their progeny also engaged in this
type of salvific behavior. Indeed one suspects that
there may be great numbers of specific messages
and instructions that genetic tissue in the different
species holds for the survival of progeny.

Reports have it that certain fish can be conditioned through a reward and punishment system
to move toward an object of a particular color
placed in their aquarium. If, for instance, they
move toward what we see as a red object, they are
rewarded with food. If, on the other hand, they
move to touch a green object, they are given a mild
electric shock. Such conditioning is re-enforced
through hundreds of applications. Then fish so
conditioned are removed from the aquarium and
killed; their brains are powdered and mixed with
fish food that is fed to another group of their
species that has not been conditioned to respond to
color. This second group of fish eventually begin to
behave in the same way that the initial group did.
Some experimenters have concluded that the conditioning produced in the nervous tissue of the first
group of fish was somehow preserved in its molecular structure, and communicated to the second
group, eventually to make itself felt again in their
behavior patterns. If all of this is indeed true, then
it is easy to see how behavior, particularly characteristic ways of responding to certain stimuli, can
be introduced in some coded way not merely into
the genetic but even into the somatic tissue of
certain species of animals.

In the Serengeti Plain of East Africa every year

thousands upon thousands of wildebeest bear their young. At first the infants are extremely weak and unable even to stand. But within a few minutes they rise to their feet, wobbly and unsteady at first, but with a rapidly increasing agility, until eventually they are able to walk with a measured step around their mothers in search of nourishment. Within a half-hour the tiny wildebeest is able to run and accompanies its mother when she rejoins the herd. Within an hour it is able to keep up with the herd. Its sudden growth to maturity in this particluar area of its development has to utterly amaze one.

The length of time that it takes the young of any species to acquire such characteristics as one is wont to associate with the adults of that species, and consequently to be able to survive without assistance from adults, is called neoteny. Some animals, like the wildebeest and grazing animals in general have a relatively short neoteny. Others, like human infants, have a long neoteny; in fact human infants enjoy a neoteny that is among the longest in all the animal kingdom. Indeed there is hardly another species in which the young are so totally dependent upon their parents for survival. The human infant is totally and absolutely helpless. In fact, this abject dependence of the human infant upon adults for survival prompted one of the early colleagues of Sigmund Freud, the renowned Otto Rank, to advance his theory of the birth trauma.

According to Rank, the human infant in the uterus enjoys absolutely perfect security and is completely free from any kind of anxiety since all its needs are adequately provided for. But at birth it is suddenly ejected from this comfortable and cozy environment and thrust into one that it experiences as tremendously hostile. Only with the care and assistance of its parents or other adults will it be able to survive in this alien territory. According to Rank, the fact that we do not remember our birth is not due to the fact that we were not sufficiently conscious to experience it, but to the fact that we did experience it as the worst of all threats to our existence — we experienced in no ordinary way our mortality — and simply repressed the memory. Rank's theory proposes that every time we are involved with change in our life situation, especially at the time we leave home for school, enter into adolescence, commit ourselves to the married life, and so forth, the specter of the birth trauma haunts us. We are not able to recognize it as such. We are not really able to cope with it. And so we are very likely to respond in neurotic or psychotic ways — and these may become a characteristic way of handling the new situation.

Because of the unusually long period of neoteny the human infant is perforce egocentric. To survive it must continually call attention to itself, to its basic needs. It must strive with all the ability it has to focus the attention of others upon its exigencies. So it naturally tends to become very self-centered. It cannot help this. It is simply part of its genetic inheritance, necessary to assure its survival. Geneticists might say that in primitive times only those infants survived who were able to call attention to their needs, who were able to impress upon their parents the necessity of responding to their cries and other expressions of distress. Together with the natural instincts of its mother, the infant's proclivity to attract attention to itself, to be fully and completely preoccupied with ego needs, assured its success in the grim business of staying alive. This instinct for survival is strong in the young of any species. But the more the sense of dependence, the greater it becomes. The selfishness that ensues from this tendency may well constitute the radical alienation from the basically altruistic attitude that must characterize human society in general if it is to live in accordance with God's precepts, all of which are rooted in love of others. The extraordinarily strong survival instinct of the human infant, now an inherited trait, brings about a disorientation both from that condition or status which human adult society finds most beneficial for its well-being, and from common goals which alone can assure security and peace among groups of men. Thus right from the beginning, from the preconscious state of the human individual, he is inclined to what the theologian would call sin. He has inherited a tendency to deviate from the good, from what is loving of others, from what is altruistic. Thus from the time of his birth, from the very inception of his life outside the womb he leans toward what will eventually become the attitude he will carry throughout his life unless something intervenes: to prefer himself rather than his neighbor.

Likely, as man emerged from prehominid forms,

there was already in vogue a relatively long period
of neoteny with consequent genetic development of
egocentric tendencies. This condition affected the
emergent self-reflective person so that he began to
behave in a sinful manner and to experience guilt.
The theologian would believe that the actual event-
uation of this was precluded by divine intervention.
God's grace was bestowed upon mankind initially
to stave off the results of this natural proclivity.
But, through some fault of his, primitive man was
alienated from God and lost for himself and his
progeny this precious gift. Man was no longer a
friend of God. All of the various human stocks became alienated. Sin is infectious, cottoning as it
does to man's primitive tendency to selfishness. But
of course, neither the scientist nor the theologian
has any really specific information about emergent
man. Neither can tell us exactly what happened. In
the mythical account of the fall of man in Christian
and Jewish revelation the act of eating a forbidden
fruit symbolizes a radical disobedience which
primitive man manifested toward his divine bene-
factor. Mention of the influence of the devil upon
this action might well point to an ancient story, also
reflected in the creation accounts of other religions,
that primitive man was led astray by aliens, by
creatures from another world.

This view of original sin has the distinct advantage of providing reasonable compliance with the
stipulations of the Council of Trent, and thus
allows for a true interface between Roman Catholic

theology and science without any compromise on either side. It acknowledges a hereditary alienation from God. Mankind is worse off in body and soul than it would have been had God's offer of friendship not been rejected. Man is left in his natural condition; his purely natural functioning as man is not impaired or lessened; he has freedom of choice between good and evil, though he is inclined to selfishness in his options. This hypothesis makes man stand in need of God's grace, not to accomplish the good in individual cases, but to perform salvific acts and in the long run to turn out as a good person, worthy of an eternal reward. This grace is made possible of attainment for man through the sacrifice of Jesus. He is the new source of grace, and so can be regarded as the head of a new race of men, human beings who are able because of him to rise above the trammels of sinful existence and live in friendship and love with God and their fellows.

Of course it can be objected that just because modern infants have a long neoteny, it does not mean that primitive ones did too. While certainly this is true, it would seem unlikely that emergent man's young would not remain dependent for a relatively long time, because this seems to be a characteristic of primates in general, and not merely of man. Moreover, the argumentation does not depend primarily upon the actual length of neoteny in humans, but rather on the self-reflective experience of total dependence. The longer, of course, that experience is sustained, the likelier it is

to produce a more immediate effect upon the
genes.

If this hypothesis survives scrutiny by scientist
and theologian alike, it will serve to bypass the
problem created by the postulate of polygenetic
evolution, one that, as we have seen, has been a
challenge to those theologians who wish to remain
in full accord with their tradition.

Chapter VI

ANGELS AND DEVILS

THEOLOGY and science alike affirm the existence of intelligent creatures other than human beings in the universe.

Angels have always been an important component of both Jewish and Christian theology. The Christian theologian calls angels purely spiritual beings. Their reality bears a similarity to that of the human soul or spirit. While the human soul remains in itself radically independent of matter for its existence, in this life it can operate only with the material element, the body, of which Scholastic philosophy predicates it to be the form. In this present life the human soul cannot function without the cooperation of the material body. Angels, on the other hand, are pure spirits. Both their existence and operation are totally independent of any earthly material reality. They do not possess an earthly body. Like the human soul they enjoy immortality. Since they, too, are spirits, they are not composed of any parts that can disintegrate. They possess an intellect and a will. And they can be good or evil, depending on how they orientate their existence in relation to God's law. They occupy no particular area of space; they can move about instantaneously in all of creation. The famous question as to how many of them could

133

exist on the head of a pin is hardly disputed in
theology today; if it has to be answered, theologians would undoubtedly say legions of them. But
few people who believe in their existence would
contest the fact that they can make their presence
felt by the effects they can produce on material
creation.

The writings of so-called Pseudo-Dionysius the
Areopagite list nine choirs of angels. These distrib-
ute themselves, three each, into three orders. The
first order contains the seraphim, the cherubim and
the thrones in the order of their precedence and
dignity before God. Highest of all the angels are the
seraphim. The second order comprises domina-
tions, virtues and powers. The third order encompasses principalities, archangels and angels.
Thomas Aquinas taught that each angel, unlike the
creatures we are familiar with, constitutes a distinct
species unto itself. There are no subspecies or individuals among the angelic hosts.

Scripture insinuates that the angels were put to
some kind of test, just as man was, with reference
to their loyalty to God. As the story goes, the most
prestigious of the seraphs, Lucifer, led a revolt
against the Lord. So in angelic mythology Lucifer
and his followers became devils. The bad angels or
devils try to thwart the Lord in his plans for man.
Strictly speaking, devils ought to be distinguished
from condemned human souls who are more properly called demons, but mostly the words "demon"
and "devil" are used interchangeably. Sometimes

Lucifer, the prince of the devils, is referred to as Satan, at other times simply as *the* devil.

The Bible gives us the names of some of the angels. There is the archangel Michael, whose name poses a question: "Who is like God?" Thus the very name of this archangel taunts Lucifer whose sin of pride indicates that he fancied himself to be like God. Tradition says that Michael was the one responsible for casting Lucifer into hell. What a humiliation for the mighty seraph Lucifer to be deprived of glory by one of such an inferior order, and one whose own name mocks the ambition of the prince of darkness. Then there is Gabriel, whose name praises the strength of the Lord. And Raphael, the healing power or medicine of the Lord. And others whose names single out certain attributes or powers of the divinity.

Traditional theology acknowledges that God has assigned a twofold role to angels. First, angels act as messengers between God and mankind. Thus they take a very active part in salvation history. In fact the word "angel" is taken from the Greek word meaning "messenger." In the Old Testament angels often stood as intermediaries between Yahweh and his people, bringing them his advice, his promises, his challenges, his rebukes. The prophets also did this, but when angels assumed this role it is sometimes difficult to distinguish them from Yahweh himself, for in certain cases the Hebrew word that is translated in our versions as "angel" could in the context really signify some kind of appearance of Yahweh himself. So for the Hebrew an angel was a grand and glorious being, much like Yahweh himself.

The second role assumed by angels at the direction of the Lord is that of guarding human beings and their societies from the power of the devil. The doctrine relating to guardian angels has impregnated the prayer life and liturgy of the Church, perhaps more in the past than in the present, but there still remains an acknowledgement of it in the official ritual of the Church.

Traditional theology assigns to the devils the role of populating hell with human beings. They accomplish this by bringing men to lead sinful lives. Theologians have singled out three ways by which this onslaught is carried out. First — and this is the principal way devils relate to humans — they tempt us. This means that they invite or entice us in various ways to commit sin. Secondly, at times they invade our privacy even more atrociously by obsessing us. This means that they continuously harass us, wear us down until we yield to their sinful suggestions. Obsession is very much like temptation except that it is more intense, unrelenting and continued indefinitely. Thirdly, devils possess human beings. This is actually the worst thing a devil can do to us. When a person is possessed the devil enters his body and takes charge of its activity. He uses it often to manifest his magical power as an angel. The human soul still remains the form of that body, but it is paralyzed; it is no longer in control. The devil directs the activities of a possessed human being. Thus he attempts by his displays to frighten other humans to yield to him.

Some theologians wonder whether today Christians have to believe anymore in the doctrine about the existence of angels and devils. Noting the ambiguity about the use of the word "angel" in the Old Testament, they ask could angels just be theophanies, that is, appearances of God himself, objectifications of him in our consciousness? Could devils be mere personifications of human ills, problems and tendencies? Could the devils mentioned in Scripture be primitive personifications of psychological or psychosomatic diseases which in ancient times were left undiagnosed?

Theologians agree that the most important Council to deal with the issue of an angelic world was the fourth one held at the Lateran palace in Rome in 1215. Up until that time Councils and other authorities did deal with the issue of angels and devils, but their existence seemed to be taken for granted. Belief in an invisible creation had not in any significant way been challenged. But at the time of the Fourth Lateran Council the relationship of that invisible creation to human self-understanding in accordance with the Gospel message was called into question. The Council actually made no significant changes in the traditional view, but merely affirmed the fact that matter, too, held its place in creation, that it was good but corruptible.

The Council of Nicaea in 325 issued a profession of faith that relegates all being, both visible and invisible, under the creative mantle of God. In doing this it merely repeated notions that were included in earlier professions of faith. The Christian believes that God is the creator of whatever exists, and belief in an invisible reality is presupposed. The First Council of Constantinople in 381 sets forth the same doctrine. Around this time Manichaean heretics had taught that there was a twofold creative principle, a god of good and a god of evil. The good god created spirits, the invisible creation. The evil god created matter, the visible creation. Earlier councils had, as we have seen, held to the position that there is only one God who brought forth from nothing both the visible and invisible creation. It only remained for Constantinople I to reiterate this teaching.

Some doubt exists as to whether Pope Vigilius actually confirmed the fifteen anathemata taken from the letter of the Emperor Justinian and levelled against the disciples of Origen through the action of the Patriarch Menas in the Fifth Ecumenical Council. Whether or not the confirmation of the pope was forthcoming, the anathemata do represent the mind of the Church at that time. Condemned was the idea that angels possess some kind of earthly body. No distinction among the different orders of angels should be made on the basis of different kinds of matter they assumed after their primordial fall from grace. Human souls cannot become angels, nor can angels be transformed into human souls. It is erroneous to consider Christ to have been some kind of angel when he appeared on earth. Nor did Christ assume an angelic nature in order to save the angels. In end-time men will not recover their purely spiritual nature through some kind of union with the divine Logos similar to that which Christ assumed while he was on earth.

The Third Council of Constantinople, in its condemnation of Origenist doctrine clearly indicated that, since angels are pure spirits, they are immortal and incorruptible. The Second Council of Nicaea in 787 affirmed once again that angels have no bodies, that is ones composed of earthly material, but permitted a discussion of opinions suggesting that they might be composed of non-earthly matter. Some of the Council fathers and theologians felt that it was necessary to circumscribe angels with some kind of body for they had to be clearly distinguished from God, whose being alone is totally spiritual and simple. But such a body could in no way be an earthly one. It had to be essentially invisible, ethereal, tenuous, perhaps in some way like what we moderns would call energy quanta.

The idea that angels have some kind of body seems substantiated by Scripture itself. The seraphim attendant upon Yahweh have wings and faces — yes, and even genitals! Of their six wings only two are used for flying; two are used to cover their faces and two to cover their genitals — Old Testament scholars tell us that the word "feet" that appears in Isaiah [6/2] is a bowdlerism for genitals.

In 1215 the twelfth ecumenical council, the fourth to be held at the Lateran palace in Rome, had as its objective the condemnation of Catharism rampant at the time in southern France. Catharism

was an offshoot of the basic Manichaean view of
creation, transmitted down through the centuries
from more remote areas through the agency of
Paulicians, Bogomils and Patarenes. For the
Catharists or Albigenses, as they were sometimes
called (although Toulouse and not Albi seemed to
be regarded as their home base) there were two
gods, one good and the other evil, the good god
producing spirit and the evil one matter.

The objective of the profession of faith issued by
the Fourth Lateran Council was to reaffirm in the
clearest possible terms the definition pronounced
initially at Nicaea: that there exists only one God,
and that he is the creator of all being, visible and invisible, material as well as spiritual. The Council
taught most strenuously that if any creature was
perceived by man as evil, that evil was due to its
own free activity. As it issued forth from the
creative hand of God it was good. Scripture vividly
points out that God creates only what is good, not
what is evil. The refrain in the creation epic shows
that God saw that all his creation was good. There
is only one God. He is the principle of all created
being. By his omnipotence at the beginning of time
he brought forth from nothingness both a spiritual
and a material creation, an angelic host and an
earthly horde. In the last phase of creation he
brought into being man who is the epitome of creation, consisting as he does of both spiritual and cor-
poral elements and thus participating in both great
orders of being. Mankind too is basically good, like
all other creatures of God — but, of course, man

has a free will which can lead him into evil. Even the devil and the angelic hosts that followed him are, inasmuch as they are creatures of God, naturally good. They became evil on their own, not because God had anything to do with their deviation from what is proper. God gave to them, as he did to man, a free will, and thus opened the way for them to sin. Through the devil's suggestion man also sinned and thus lost God's grace.

Today, I suspect, there are not a great number of theologians who would deny that the decrees of the Fourth Lateran Council are not intended to be a dogmatic definition. In the past, however, they tended to consider that the definitions were of a much wider scope than they actually were in the opinion of more recent experts. The older view held that the Council defined that whatever exists does so because it was created by the one and only God. Purely spiritual beings do exist. No creature could be like God, existing from all eternity; creatures began to exist in time. Some of God's invisible creation turned to evil ways and eventually became the cause of man's sinful activity.

In addition to these defined doctrines, theologians of yore listed a number of propositions that were to be considered theologically certain as a result of the teaching of the Council. Angels are pure spirits. By the time this Council was held, the older opinion that angels could be composite beings, consisting of spirit and some kind of nonearthly, ethereal matter had been gradually abandoned and had fallen into desuetude. Theologians, however, did not see their way to stating that this older opinion had been clearly condemned as a result of the teaching of Fourth Lateran. Much less would they hold that the later opinion of St. Bonaventure and the Scotist school, namely that angelic nature has to be physically composite, was precluded by the teaching of the Council. Of course, angelic nature has to be carefully distinguished from the divine nature: there must be at least a real distinction of some sort between essence and existence; angels do not, like God, necessarily exist. Some theologians also posited a real distinction between angelic substance on the one hand and its faculties of intellect and will on the other.

We encounter even greater disputes when we consider the Council's words: *"simul ab initio temporis"* — together from the beginning of time. There is a tradition that time began with the creation of the universe, with the creation of matter. But were angels created at that same time? Is this what the Council is teaching? Some would say that angels were created before matter, and that the phrase used by the Council does not refer to time at all, but merely to the fact that both angels and matter were created from nothing, and so to the human way of thinking, there was a time when they did not exist. Others would say that angels and the universe were created at the same time — this is the clear teaching of the Council. And so the dispute is carried on. Nor do theologians have a definite idea as to the place where the angels were created. Was it in heaven? On the earth before men inhabited it? On some other planet? In the universe at large? In some other dimensional system?

Lately a growing number of theologians seem to be of the opinion that the decree *Firmiter* of the Fourth Lateran Council in no way intended to define the *existence* of an angelic creation. Many teach that any dogmatic definition ought not to be extended beyond the scope of the error it is intended to refute. With reference to the Fourth Lateran Council, aimed as it was at the Catharists, only these notions seems to be questions of faith: first, that whatever reality exists apart from the one and only God, exists because of this creative action; there can be no act of creation apart from this God; secondly, whatever of that creation has become sinful or evil in the eyes of man has done so through its own agency; God is not involved at all.

There are no dogmatic definitions apart from these two. All other belief positions are simply affirmations of what was commonly accepted in the culture of the times. They form only background illumination in the light of which the definitions are to be understood. One cannot doubt that at the time of the definitions all orthodox believers, as well as the Catharists whose false doctrines were to be condemned in the Council, acknowledged the existence of angels, that they denied that these purely spiritual beings had a body similar to that of human beings, that they considered them to be superior to men, that they served as guardians for mankind, and that some of them had turned bad and were the enemies of earthlings, seeking to lead them into sin. These persuasions formed a theology of the times, an acculturation, that was presupposed in the Council, and confirmed by its decrees to the extent that it formed the backdrop out of which its definitions emanated, but in no way was it precisely an object of those definitions. There was no need to define what everybody accepted — heretics themselves not excluded. Similarly, hardly anyone would say that it was the intention of the Fourth Lateran Council to define as a dogma of faith the existence of the material world as we know it. In those times, as today, the existence of the world was taken for granted. When the council mentions that God is the creator of this material world, the object of the definition is the creative act of the one and only God, not the existence of the material world. *A pari*, when the Council refers to God as the creator of the invisible world, the object of the definition is the fact that that world, too, was created by the one and only God, not precisely the existence of that world. Like that of the material world, the existence of the angelic world was in those days simply taken for granted.

The decree *Sacrosancta Romana Ecclesia* issued in the reconciliation process for the Syrian Jacobites at the Council of Florence in 1442 does not shed much more light on the issue. It proposes that all creatures, since they are limited beings, are changeable. Only God is absolutely immutable. So it offers some explanation of why the angels who turned bad, even though they were perfect as they issued forth from the creative hand of God, could embrace the sinful way. Wherever one encounters limited being, one discovers that vacillation is possible. Angels are no exception; some of them became evil. But this did not in any way vitiate what they are in themselves, in their very being, in their nature. Their being remains good; only their intention, their will has deviated from what is right. It is like the case of the sinful human being; he remains basically good in himself, but his intentions and actions are evil.

The Council of Florence shows itself to be a bit more liberal than the Fourth Lateran Council in addressing itself to the question of the time when the angels were created. It seems to propose that God did not necessarily create spirit and matter at the same time. This Council seems to be very sensitive to the freedom God enjoyed in creation; it emphasizes the fact that he made both the visible and the invisible creation when he wanted to.

The dogmatic constitution *Dei Filius* of the First Vatican Council injects a new element into the traditional teaching about angels, while otherwise reiterating almost word for word the ideas set forth by the Fourth Lateran Council. Vatican I points out that in the act of creation God did not acquire anything for himself, or enlarge in any way what he already had. It indicates that his motive in creating both the visible and invisible worlds was simply to manifest his own goodness outside of himself. It was the very goodness of God himself that was imparted to his creatures, but seemingly in some analogous way, since what he gave to his creatures was not an emanation from his own being, nor did it diminish him in any way. Once again this Council takes for granted the existence of an invisible creation. Its second canon does affirm the existence of a reality other than the material, and some might tend to take it as a dogmatic pronouncement about the existence of angels. But certainly it could refer only to the human soul, which the Church has always considered immaterial; if any non-material reality exists the canon remains pertinent and valid. To conclude that it refers to angels without any specific mention of them is totally unwarranted. Then, too, theologians today are inclined not to regard canons issued by the various councils as dogmatic definitions, but rather as legal formulations that reflect but do not necessarily present the doctrinal positions sustained by the council fathers.

The encyclical *Humani generis* of Pope Pius XII, as we have already stated, treats of certain theological problems that arose in the middle of the twentieth century. One of those issues specifically handled by the encyclical was whether matter differs essentially from spirit and whether angels really are personal beings. Questions like this arise, the encyclical states, from an imprudent zeal for souls (the excess of a good thing), or from false science. It clearly was not the intention of this encyclical to issue any dogmatic pronouncements, but merely to call the attention of theologians to some of the most recent aberrations from traditional

Catholic teaching. Even modern theologians must be mindful of traditional teaching. Once again in this encyclical the fact of the existence of angels is not the direct object of the warning; it is simply presumed.

In his so-called "Credo of the People of God," Pope Paul VI, in 1968, affirmed his belief in a creator God who produced things visible "such as this world in which our transient life passes," as well as things invisible, "such as pure spirits which are also called angels." In this document there seems to be a more direct affirmation of the existence of angels, but the "Credo" seems in no sense to be a dogmatic pronouncement, but merely a restatement of traditional theological positions.

Belief in the existence of devils may be even better attested than that of angels in Holy Scripture. Jesus seems continually to be jousting with them in his public ministry. It begins with a contestation in the desert, and ends with Satan's entrance into the heart of Judas. It is peppered with victories over possessors of human victims. The official teachings of the Catholic Church make countless references to devils and consider them to be personal beings, not just the personification of human ills. They are the part of the angelic creation that went bad.

In a letter to Bishop Turibius as well as in a profession of faith that he wanted administered to all who would be consecrated bishops, Pope Leo I affirmed that the devil was indeed good as he issued forth from the creative power of God. He became evil through his own agency. In another letter to Bishop Flavianus this same pope refers to the devil as the ruler of the kingdom of death.

While some of the followers of Origen have held that the devil's punishment in hell would be gradually diminished until the end of time when he would be restored to his original status as the chief of the angels, the Synod of Constantinople in 543 counteracted by stating that his situation in hell is eternal, and that he can never be rehabilitated.

In 561, the Council of Braga in Portugal inveighed against the Manichaean and Priscillianist heretics, condemning the idea that the devil created flesh. The Council taught that evil spirits are in no way involved in the conception of a human being. It reiterates the doctrine that originally the devil was a good angel.

As was stated before, the Fourth Lateran Council insists that God can produce only what is good. The bad angels became evil on their own. Man sinned because he yielded to the temptation of the devil.

The Council of Florence proposed that no one can be freed from the power of the devil except through faith in Jesus Christ and through the reception of the sacrament of baptism.

The Council of Trent located the sinner in the devil's kingdom, a kingdom of death. The sinner remains under the power and spell of the devil and of death.

The jocular reply, "the devil made me do it," is not valid according to Pope Innocent XI in his condemnation of Quietism in 1684. The Quietists taught that a person in deep meditation or contemplation might be able to abdicate responsibility for any sinful actions and blame them on the devil. The decree of the Holy Office of the Inquisition of August 28, 1687, singling out some of the errors of Miguel Molinos points out that it is wrong to hold that in order to humiliate good persons and bring them to even higher degrees of perfection God permits devils to do violence to their bodies and make them commit seemingly sinful acts. It is an abomination to think that God would employ the ministry of devils or demons to do his work, to bring human souls to perfection. A similar opinion found in the writings of Antonio Rosmini was condemned by Pope Leo XIII.

Regarding the question of the existence of devils, we find that the same condition obtains as in the case of angels. Their existence is simply taken for granted and presupposed when statements are made about them. Nor do the documents seem to insist on the idea that devils are real persons, and not just personifications of the ills that afflict mankind. This, too, is taken for granted. Only a relatively recent group of theologians have dared to advance the opinion that devils may really not be persons at all but only personifications.

In summary, then, we can set forth the position of the Roman Catholic Church under the following headings:

1. There have been two dogmatic statements, two definitions of doctrine relative to the case in

point: a. Whatever exists outside of God exists because it was created by the one and only God; b. Whatever in creation has become evil in the estimation of men has done so through its own agency: it was totally good when it issued forth from the creative hand of God.

2. The teaching of the Church has presupposed a popular belief in the existence of angels as well as devils. Both are purely spiritual beings. Angels are good spirits. Devils are evil spirits. This popular belief had led theologians to conclude that the existence of angels and devils is a matter of Catholic belief, though not defined as such.

3. This teaching has, without going into exact detail, specified that these creatures differ essentially from the material reality that we know on earth, and that they bear a kind of similarity to human souls inasmuch as they, too, are spiritual beings. Of course, theologians in the past were not able in any positive way to distinguish this spiritual reality from some of the elements known in modern physics, but entirely oblivious to them, elements like quarks, photons, neutrinos and antimatter particles. Would these have been considered by the ancients as spiritual realities and not as just invisible forms of matter?

4. In the writings of theologians in the past, devils seem to have less status than angels. No one denies that there is evil in the world, but with a cue from yesteryear today's theologians lean more and more toward regarding devils as personifications of that evil rather than as personal agents responsible

for a large part of it. There is not as great a tendency, even today, to treat angels as personifications. Most recently, however, the media have focussed popular interest upon the phenomenon of diabolical possession, and called attention once again to the existence of the devil as a personal reality. Indeed, if one can believe as true some of the events associated with reports of diabolical possession, an adequate account for the facts could be given only by attributing personality to the forces of evil that seem to be in operation. There is no way of explaining the sum of data by recourse to a mere concatenation of purely impersonal physical causes. Attention given to this phenomenon by their clients has at times proven embarrassing and even distressing to some rabbis, priests and ministers. They have been plagued with questions, and have been driven back to their theological textbooks, many of which prove to be altogether jejune in treating issues of this sort. Because of this popular interest it may very well develop that the past tendency to regard angels as more important than devils will be reversed in the future.

5. Past belief in the existence of angels and devils has formed an integral, but by no means essential, role in the development of certain dogmas in the Roman Catholic Church. It has very significantly influenced the devotional life of the Church. The liturgy commemorates feasts of the angels. It takes account of the ministries of angels in salvation history. There is a continuous reference in the official and private prayer-life of the Church

to the devil and his machinations, and the biblical readings selected for certain rites in the Church testify even today to the ancient and traditional belief in the existence of angels and devils.

Many scientists today exhibit an unqualified enthusiasm for the exploration of the possibility of the existence of life elsewhere in the universe. Great pressure has been placed upon the Congress of the United States to provide funding for continuous investigation of outer space in the hope of discovering there some other forms of intelligent life. In 1975, the Science Policy Research Division of the Congressional Research Service in the Library of Congress prepared a report for the Committee on Science and Technology of the U.S. House of Representatives, Ninety-Fourth Congress, First Session. The title of this report is *The Possibility of Intelligent Life Elsewhere in the Universe.* It has gone through innumerable printings, and the public is still very much interested in it. The report justifies continued spending of the taxpayers' money in the hope of contacting such intelligent forms of life as are presumed to exist elsewhere throughout the universe.

In his covering letter to the Honorable Don Fuqua, chairman of the Subcommittee on Space Science and Applications, Norman Beckman of the Library of Congress indicates that recent hearings in the Congressional subcommittee, headed by Representative Fuqua, on the future of the space program have raised questions about why we are spending so much money on manned and unmanned junkets into space. It was remarked that during the hearings, a number of witnesses commented upon the possibility of intelligent life existing outside of our solar system, and insinuated that we ought to try to communicate with such creatures, if indeed they do exist. The group noted that this subject is receiving more and more attention among scientists not only in this country, but in the Soviet Union, as well, where experts have already drawn up and published an outline of a research program directed toward this goal.

The report relates how, under the auspices of the National Academy of Sciences in November, 1961, an American group of distinguished persons met at Greenbank, West Virginia to study the issue of the probability of intelligent life elsewhere in the universe. The eleven prominent scientists who attended this meeting represented the fields of communications, chemistry, physics, astrophysics, astronomy, biology and animal behavior. What resulted from the meeting was the publication of a formula to ascertain the probability of the existence of intelligent life beyond the earth. The now famous Greenbank formula as it is called is written as follows:

$$N = Rf_p n_e f_l f_i f_c L$$

where the symbols designate the following:

N is the number of extant civilizations possessing currently both the interest in and capability for some kind of interstellar communication;

R is the mean rate of star formation averaged over the lifetime of a galaxy;

f_p is the fraction of stars with planetary systems;

n_e is the mean number of planets in each planetary system with an environment favorable for the origin of life;

f_l is the fraction of suitable planets on which life does develop;

f_i is the fraction of life-bearing planets on which intelligent life might appear;

f_c is the fraction of planets in which an advanced technical civilization might evolve;

L is the lifetime of a technical civilization, and this was the most difficult variable to establish.

Because of differences of opinion as to the various factors, particularly R, the rate of star formation, between Carl Sagan and the rest of the group, two numerical outcomes resulted. The majority felt that the lowest number of civilizations would be 40 and that the upper limit would be 50,000,000. Carl Sagan said that the lowest number would be 10, and the highest one million. Thus the group opined that there could be any number of civilizations, ranging from 10 to 50,000,000, that would currently have the capability of communicating in some way or other with us. The significant point, though, one which many people would not have considered likely, is that all these distinguished scientists agreed that there are at least 10 such civilizations. There is no doubt that this information was instrumental in the appropriation of vast sums of money for the space program in the attempt to communicate with these intelligent creatures somewhere out in space.

In 1960, Dr. Frank Drake of the National Radio Astronomy Laboratory inaugurated a program that was dubbed "Operation Ozma." Scientists listened for over 200 hours, trying to pick up radio signals from two stars, Tau Ceti and Epsilon Eridani, both about 11 light years from the earth. They listened to a radio tuned to 1420 megahertz, the characteristic frequency of hydrogen, the most abundant element in the universe. They hoped to pick up some signal that might indicate that there was intelligent life in the vicinity of these stars. But the operation was a failure.

NASA Research Center in conjunction with Stanford University conducted, in 1971, a pilot design for a system to intercept radio messages from outer space. This endeavor was called "Operation Cyclops." The group involved assayed to design and set up a vast array of antennae that would be able to pick up faint signals from star systems as far away as 100 light years. They contemplated using as many as 1000 antennas for the pickup. This would require a collecting area that would encompass up to twenty square kilometers of land. The installation would be more than ten times larger than the antenna system at Aricebo in Puerto Rico. Thus far no action has been taken on this proposal; it remains in the design stage.

On November 16, 1974, earthlings sent out their first message from the Aricebo observatory operated by Cornell University and the National Science Foundation in Puerto Rico. Coded information was sent out from a huge antenna and aimed at a cluster of stars approximately 24,000 light years from earth. This means that it would take 48,000 years to get any reply, even if the greetings were returned instantly! The message was sent out in digital form, and so presumed that anyone who might receive it would know enough to translate the dead carrier or zero into a white square in a graph, and the on-carrier or one into a black square, a code that even some smart earthlings might not be able to break. What intelligence would the alien receive if he were able to break the code? The message sent out included numbers from one to ten, formulas for sugars and bases and nucleotides of DNA, a representation of the double helix of DNA, a graphic representation of a human being, giving his average height, a numeric calculation of the human population of the earth at this time, a diagrammatic symbolization of the solar system and an outline picture of the antenna of the Aricebo radio telescope that transmitted the message.

Most people have seen a photograph of the plaque that was affixed to the Pioneer Ten space probe. At its top there is a schematic representation of the hyperfine transition between parallel and antiparallel proton and electron spins of a neutral hydrogen atom. Beneath this representation is the number one in binary code. There also is depicted the emission of a radio frequency photon about 21 centimeters in wave length, with a frequency that is characteristic of hydrogen, 1420 megahertz. It was thought that since hydrogen is the most abundant atom in the galaxy, it might be recognized and provide some rudimentary basis for communication. On the right side of the plaque a naked man and woman are represented, and at the bottom there is a diagram showing the sun and its planets with a special notation of the position of the earth in this configuration. In conjunction with earth there is a miniature line drawing of the spacecraft itself.

Similar plaques were contained in the other Pioneer and Mariner space hardware which were intended eventually to drift into the far reaches of space. Some of the Mariner craft also contained other informational materials, like recordings of earth sounds, pictures of the various races and ethnic groups of earth people, and so forth.

One has to wonder whether much of this was not a colossal waste of the taxpayers' money. Not that the basic idea was wrong. But much of the material was designed with the presupposition not only that the intelligence of other creatures would be equal or superior to ours, but that other intelligent creatures would have to have both a consciousness and an experience similar to ours here on earth. To me such a presupposition evidences a kind of racist mentality which one would hope scientists would be free of. To be intelligent, aliens have to be like us. Even the drawings or artist's conceptions of living forms elsewhere in the universe that are contained at the end of the report to Congress represent a very earthbound mentality with reference to the possible development of life in places other than the earth. We would recognize almost all of them as monstrous earth creatures; would they really be the type of creatures we would expect to encounter in a world totally different from ours? We know, for instance, that on earth there tends to be a certain consistency (statistically verifiable) within the molecular structure of each living creature. They are composed almost entirely of either levorotating or dextrorotating molecules, rarely of any combination of the two. Consequently they manifest a frontal symmetry that we recognize as characteristic of earth creatures. Look at a human being from the front and draw a line down the center. You will see a perfect balance or symmetry. Left ear will be set against right ear, left eye against right eye, left nostril against right nostril, left arm and hand against right arm and hand, left leg and foot against right leg and foot, and so forth. But now turn the human being 90° sidewise and look at him. Draw a line down the center as before and note the result. You will get no symmmetry. His nose will be set against the back of his head, his chest against his backbone, his toes against his heels. Earth creatures in higher evolutionary forms do not manifest antadiform symmetry. Yet this is no reason for saying that it could not have developed elsewhere in other evolutionary processes. If there are equal numbers of levorotating and dextrorotating molecules in the universe, and if there is a certain randomness in the selection of these in life forms, why could we not envision mixtures of the two in the development of life elsewhere that might have resulted in forms totally different from our conceptualization of earth creatures? Why, for instance, could not the sensing organs of creatures elsewhere have developed in such a way as to make them sensitive to areas in their environment that without mechanical aids we are totally oblivious to? The chief organ of our consciousness is our eye. It responds to an extremely narrow area of the spectrum. Could they have an organ that would respond not to the visible spectrum (for us) but to x-rays, or gamma rays? How would this affect their consciousness?

When we sent out the plaque that many people have seen on Pioneer Ten, we presupposed that an alien intercepting it someplace out in space would not only be able to decipher it, but would first be able to read or see it. This presupposes that he would have some organ similar to our eye that would respond to the very narrow spectrum of visible light, which ranges only from 4 to 7.2×10^{-5} centimeters. What if such a creature has only "eyes" that will respond to x-rays? He would be aware only of the dim outlines of the plastic plaque, and "see" right through the rest of it! Or suppose the chief organ of sense that feeds his consciousness responds only to gamma rays? He would be conscious only of the molecular structure which forms the basis of the plaque on which the message has been written. He could in no way "see" the message.

Thus we also seem to be off target in sending out our narrow band radio transmission from Aricebo and elsewhere. We presuppose that this miniscule needle in the gigantic haystack of electromagnetic energy will be able to be located. Think of the odds against that, even if we are dealing with creatures of an intelligence superior to our own.

Or what if this is the case? What if intelligent creatures in other areas of the universe already know of our existence, but do not care? What if they do not want to respond to our overtures? What if they have already tried to communicate with us by means our scientists would not expect them to use, and we have ignored them? What if they do not use radio or flashing lights? Would it be too fantastic to think that maybe they have tried to communicate with us in the religious experience of earth people?

Perhaps we could avoid the colossal and possibly fruitless expenditure of money if we could design a receiver that could scan very wide ranges of the spectrum of electromagnetic energy — not just the visible spectrum or the radio spectrum, but all the way from low frequency radio to cosmic rays to search for organized emissions. It would, undoubtedly, be much better if we could design a transmitter that could operate in this way, but that does not seem to be at all feasible in the present state of our technological development. Receivers use much less energy, and can be constructed at a much more reasonable cost. Such a receiver would have to have a rather astonishing array of sensing units or antennas, transducers of various types to reduce the different signals intercepted to one common channel and a computer programmed to distinguish intelligible messages from random space "noise." To think of such a project at this time would be staggering indeed. But in the long run, it might be the only really effective way of achieving our objective in the search for intelligent life in outer space.

But even if SETI (the search for extraterrestrial intelligence) has thus far netted only negative results, it is concrete evidence for one thing — the fact that scientists really do believe that there is intelligent life elsewhere in the universe. It is not entirely wasteful of money, time and effort to attempt to communicate with it even in the feeble and sometimes mindless ways that we have attempted. The fact of scientists' conviction that such life does indeed exist might allow us to put some faith in reports and stories about encounters with aliens that do not seem to be in themselves, on their own naked merits, well-documented or substantiated. If we can legitimately presuppose that extraterrestrial intelligent life does indeed exist, and that it might well have the possibility of communication with us, some phenomena that have hitherto remained very mysterious could possibly be given some explanation.

I have said that our space probes thus far have been faulted by what I can best term a racist mentality, that is, they presuppose that all intelligent creatures, if indeed they are intelligent, must be like us. They must have a consciousness like ours, have sensing organs like ours, be able to appreciate various aspects of the universe the way we appreciate them, and revel in the same kind of Boolean logic we prize so much. If, however, an incident reported by a British science writer, Duncan Lunan, is true, and has been accurately analyzed by current investigators, it would give some evidence that alien intelligence might, unlike ours, be totally unprejudiced. It would put us to shame. It would manifest a truly angelic intelligence. For this attempt at contact with earth could have been one made by aliens who showed a desire to communicate with us on our terms, not their own.

It all began back in the pioneering days of radio. Experimenters were using a radar-like device to measure accurately the distance between the earth and the moon at a particular time of the year. Basically radar consists of a transmitter from which a dish-like antenna sends out a short pulse at an extremely high frequency. The transmitter phase of the operation then ceases briefly and the antenna is used as a listening device to receive back the reflected pulse transmitted in the previous phase. A timing device between the transmitter and receiver permits an accurate measurement of the elapsed time between the two phases: just when the pulse is emitted and when the return pulse arrives at the receiver. By knowing that radio waves travel at a speed of approximately 186,420 miles per second, it is possible to determine the distance of an object from the transmitting source. By timing the flight out and back of the radar pulse, dividing by two and multiplying by 186,420 the distance in miles of the moon from the earth could be obtained. Now we know that the mean distance of the moon from the earth is about 238,860 miles. So the elapsed time from the transmitting phase to the reception of the reflected pulse should have been roughly 2.56 seconds. At first it was. But then a strange thing happened. Observers began to note a varied time interval, one that was always considerably less than the expected one, but which varied considerably. They checked their instrument and could not detect any malfunction. Puzzled, they logged very carefully in their record of this experiment exactly what took place. They could not explain what they had encountered but felt that whatever it was might be important for the future of the equipment.

Scientists today guess that the following scenario might well offer an explanation for the strange incident of the wayward radar. Interposed somewhere out in space, between the earth and its moon, was an alien space probe. On board was very sensitive electromagnetic equipment that was designed to scan an extremely wide area of the spectrum and a computer capable of detecting organized transmissions and distinguish them from the random energies prevalent in space, and then to direct the probe and vector it to intercept those transmissions, and finally to absorb those transmissions and broadcast on exactly the same frequency a pre-programmed message giving information about the origin of the probe. The openness of the probe in the first instance evidences a lack of prejudice that has to be a clear indicator of the intelligence of its designer. The versatility of the probe in the absorption and rebroadcasting of a signal on exactly the same frequency received is an additional factor to be considered. This probe, even if our analysis is not correct, at least provides factors to be considered in our design efforts. If it is indeed real, then it has to be a model for us.

What was the message of this alien space probe? Scientists today have plotted the different temporal intervals transmitted by the probe on a graph so that they could be converted into spatial differentials. Superimposing one of our charts of the heavens upon it, we find that the only one that fits perfectly is the one associated with the double star system Epsilon Boötis. Thus, translated into English (obviously then we are inserting our perspective: we could not know from the data supplied what the aliens call their system in their own language) the message would read: "This is a space probe from the sixth planet of the double star system, Epsilon Boötis."

The use of such high technology in a space probe would indicate that, if indeed this is a message from aliens, even at the beginning of our twentieth century, their intelligence would have been greatly superior to ours, so much so that at that time we

were unable to understand or translate their
message and understand what they were trying to
do. Why such probes do not attempt to contact us
today when we would be in a better position to appreciate them is quite problematic. Perhaps that
probe was just a test to find out how advanced
technologically we were. When no response on our
part was made, a conclusion might have been
drawn that we were unable to respond, and an attempt to communicate once again deferred for who
knows how long a time?

This is not to say that today we do not from time
to time detect signals that have to be distinguished
from the random ones emanating from outer space,
signals that seem to have an intelligent origin. But
these signals are invariably traced back to an
earthly source. Usually they are found to have been
produced by the military or other classified or semi-
classified transmitters. The current relative silence
of alien intelligence has led a few scientists to
surmise that any civilizations that do exist out in
space simply have not as yet reached a level of technology that would enable them to communicate
with us. On the other hand, many opine that alien
technology is so superior to ours that the directors
of their communications programs would consider
us too primitive even to warrant an attempt at contact. They know we would not understand and be
able to respond; they do not really know how far
we have advanced in the past twenty years. It is this
second view that keeps SETI funded.

Another group of writers like Erich von

Däniken, whose ideas have been seriously challenged by a number of scientists, claims to have found evidences of alien visitation in the past on the face of the earth itself. One of the most spectacular is the markings on the Nazca Plain in Peru. Here one encounters what appear to be a gigantic array of figures representing spiders, birds, snakes and flowers, some of them twice as large as a football field, impressed into the terrain of this particular basin in South America. In addition to these figures there are mysterious lines, some of them 40 miles in length. What is amazing, of course, is that from the earth these drawings cannot be detected at all. Only if one goes to the mountain tops or flies over the area in an airplane do the tracings become visible as such. Some surmise that they may have served as navigational aids for alien space craft that used this area for landings sometime in the distant past. Whether this is a plausible explanation or not, it still is astounding that they could have been constructed at all. Such a maneuver could not have been executed without some direction from high above, say, from a scout placed on the top of a mountain. But without binoculars and radio communication this would have been an extremely tedious task. Some scientists are of the opinion that these landmarks could have been plotted originally on a graph, and then executed on the terrain square by square. This certainly was possible, if not too plausible when one considers the fact that the lines all match perfectly. Von Däniken suggests that these configurations may well have been made either by or under the direction of an alien force that visited the Nazca Plain many centuries ago. It may have been designed as a landing area for their space craft.

The steles at Stonehenge in England have always posed a challenge to scientists. People tend to regard them as very mysterious even today. This ancient site was used by prehistoric man even earlier than the second millenium before Christ. There do not seem to be any definite answers as to who was responsible for the phenomenon, how it came to be, or what its precise purpose was. It is known that the site was rebuilt around 1500 B.C. Notable in the pile of stones is a huge boulder which had to be brought in from 24 miles away. Other rocks in the edifice were brought from much farther. On the site are some 56 pits which have been called Aubrey Holes. Some have associated Stonehenge with Druid worship, but it would seem that the site was well-established long before the arrival of the Druids in England. The British researcher Gerald Hawkins has advanced the best theory to date to account for the phenomenon. He proposes that Stonehenge was simply a gigantic calendar elaborated in stone, a calendar used in conjunction with an astronomical observatory. He points out that when one stands at a particular spot in the center of the edifice the sun as well as the moon and certain stars appear in consistent patterns that cannot be merely coincidental. In one area the moon rises over a particular stone in mid-winter in a cycle of about 18½ years. Other observations have been made in regard to other astronomical bodies. All the mathematical calculations and astronomical data have been verified by computer analysis, and proven to be very accurate — unusually accurate for the time. The conclusion of all this might be either that what researchers have projected into the phenomenon of Stonehenge is a lot more than the facts warrant, or that the accuracy of the data cannot be accounted for by what we know to have been the mathematical and technological status of civilization at the time that the site was constructed. In the latter case the facts can be explained only by recurring to well-informed outside sources that assisted primitive man in the construction and use of the materials. Could those outside sources have been aliens with an advanced technology?

The accuracy of the Mayan calendar poses a similar problem. No doubt the Mayans founded a relatively sophisticated culture and a well organized society in Central America long before the advent of Columbus to the New World. But still it would seem to be beyond the capabilities of this culture, advanced as it was for its time, to construct a calendar evidencing such astronomical precision. How was such a feat possible? Could the Mayans have received advice from aliens? Was the calendar itself a product of extraterrestrial visitors? How else could this rather unique phenomenon be explained?

Writers also bring our attention to bear on the massive construction job and engineering marvel that were involved in erecting the pyramids in Egypt. It would be easier to account for them if recourse could be had to some kind of outside technological assistance. In terms of sheer labor alone the task seems overwhelming. Without the help of machinery it would have taken upwards of 500,000 slaves a whole lifetime to construct just a representative number of the larger pyramids that one finds in the valley of the Nile. Theoretically, or course, this is possible, but once again some scientists think that it was unlikely. Here, too, the facts can better be accounted for if one presupposes that outside technical help was obtained.

Another interesting fact that writers like Von Däniken adduce for our consideration is the stereotyped figures of gods and heroes in the sculptures and bas reliefs emanating from ancient times, a stereotyping that is not restricted to one culture or another, but seems to be found worldwide. Small, helmeted figures with square jaws, deep-set eyes and wide shoulders are found in what are thought to be idols of gods in scattered areas of the ancient earth. They range from India through Central and South America all the way to the Mid-East. More recent examples can be found in the islands of the Pacific. And they are all basically alike. The question is bound to be asked: Could these be representations of aliens who visited the earth in ancient times and were worshiped as gods or venerated as heroes? Would the ever-present helmet, which we now recognize as characteristic of astronauts, have been part of the gear of these space travellers of yesteryear? Once again this is an interesting theory, but by no means the only plausible explanation. Memories of mankind's most primitive common past, images retained from the dawn of self-consciousness, projections from an ever more active imagination, might possibly offer a competing theory.

There are all kinds of reports of mysterious creatures roaming the backwoods and remote areas even of our modern world. We think of the rumors of the Abominable Snowman or Big Foot. But celebrated and fairly well-documented are the reports of a alien creature that haunted the English towns and countryside for a considerable amount of time during the last century. A number of eyewitnesses claim to have spotted him, and give us a general description. He wore a sort of tight-fitting white jumpsuit that seemed to emit a kind of phosphorescent glow. A fishbowl type of helmet covered his whole head. He was able to make extraordinarily sudden entrances and exits. He could jump 30 feet or more into the air. British newspapers gave eyewitness accounts, but no really satisfying explanation has ever been offered. Some of the accounts of eyewitnesses were given by those who seemed especially qualified, since they were military personnel trained to observe. Two army sentries on duty actually fired at the apparition with no apparent effect. The creature escaped from them, as they testified, by emitting a bluish-white glow and making a tremendous bound which took him over their heads and out of range of their fire in an exceptionally short time.

Reports of encounters with UFOs (unidentified flying objects) constitute another rather vast area of unexplained data. During World War II and for a while afterwards, every air force base throughout the whole world had an officer who was assigned to debrief all pilots after their various sorties and missions with reference to any encounters they might have had with UFOs. Vast amounts of materials were gathered through these routine examinations. Of course, many of the reported sightings turned out to be merely natural phenomena of one kind or another, often associated with weather fronts, which had been mistaken by pilots for UFOs. Sometimes pilots even reported other aircraft as UFOs. Even trained personnel can, admittedly, sometimes make mistakes. But apart from all of this there still remains a significant amount of seemingly genuine material that is left unexplained.

Notable in the investigation of these incidents is Professor J. Allen Hynek, an expert who admits he does not have all the answers. The Air Force eventually discontinued its surveillance of UFOs when it reassured itself and the Defense Department, after reviewing many reports and making many careful studies, that these unidentified flying objects sighted by pilots posed no threat to the security of the United States. They were evidently not sponsored by hostile aliens or any of the earthly enemies of the United States. It cost the government vast amounts of money to gather all this information, keep records of it and hire experts to analyze it. So once authorities were convinced that these invasions were friendly, or at least non-aggressive, and they would not breach our security, all these investigatory operations were discontinued. Considerable amounts of material resulting from the previous investigations still remain in storage and some of them are accessible to researchers. However, a Supreme Court decision of March 8, 1982 protected 135 of these documents that were classified as secret from UFO buffs who wanted to examine them. They were held by the National Security Agency. The high court decided that exposing them to the public gaze might give away some of the classified methods used by the government services for monitoring unidentified aircraft.

Even after official government tabulation of the activities of UFOs was suspended, sightings continued to be made in places as far away as Australia and Marseilles, France and as close to the heartland of the United States as Pascagoula, Mississippi.

In this last incident, which occurred on October 11, 1973, Charles Hickson, 42, and his 19-year-old partner, Calvin Parker, were fishing off an old pier in the Pascagoula River not far from a shipyard. They noted in an official police report that first they experienced a blue hazy light coming down from the sky. It got brighter and hovered over them at a very close range. The object they saw was gigantic, and they perceived it to be shaped somewhat like a fish. Three aliens got out of the ship and approached the men. They were small in stature, had wrinkled skin, claw-like hands and pointed ears. The two men were taken into the spacecraft by these creatures. They described the experience of boarding the ship as being simply floated into it in some kind of weightless condition. One of the fishermen reported that inside he was placed in front of an instrument that resembled a large eye. He felt that he was being scrutinized and examined very carefully. After this examination he was floated back to his position on the pier. The excitement of the encounter was simply too much for the other man, and apparently he remained in a state of unconsciousness during the whole time after fainting upon his initial contact with the aliens.

People who knew these two men quite well reported that they were well balanced individuals, and that their reports should be taken as reliable. After his interview with them Dr. Hynek seemed to place credence in the incident.

Widespread publicity was given to the encounter of Barney and Betty Hill with a UFO. It took place on September 19, 1961 on a road in New Hampshire. They described the incident as follows. A very bright light descended from the sky and landed near their car. Upon closer examination they were able to see lines of what looked like windows in a glowing craft which looked to them like a wingless airplane. Upon approaching the craft which now was hovering just above the earth, they saw behind the windows a large number of humanoid creatures, who were apparently intent upon viewing them. They got back in their car and drove away from the scene. On their way they became very drowsy, and diagnosed their subsequent condition as a bad case of amnesia. During a later session under hypnosis they were able to describe what had happened during their blackout. Both of them were taken aboard the spacecraft and given a thorough physical examination by the humanoid creatures. In the places where they indicated instruments had probed their bodies there later developed wart-like extrusions of skin. After the incident, the Hills regained their normal consciousness and were able to drive their car back home, but they did not remember in their conscious state what had happened after they became drowsy.

While a great deal of scepticism surrounded the story of these two people, particularly since the most exciting part of their account had to be recovered from them while they were under hypnosis, a number of experts felt that their narration was true: the Hills had a genuine encounter with aliens from a UFO. Material recovered from the subconscious while a person is in a hypnotic state is considered by many qualified individuals to be even more reliable than reports that are given in a fully conscious state.

One of the facts about UFO sightings that tends to corroborate the narrations of those who claim to have seen them is that some of them have also been tracked on radar screens. And in some cases both visual and radar observations confirm the phenomenon of an instantaneous disappearance of these objects. To disappear instantaneously from a radar screen without any trace lines at all might well indicate that a craft is moving close to the speed of light. It should take a few milliseconds for objects moving even at tremendous speeds to disappear from visual and radar range, so when blips disappear instantly without any trace one must begin to think in terms of speeds that are almost unimaginable on earth, or else invite speculation that such a craft might have passed through a warp into another dimensional system.

The idea that intelligent aliens may actually come from another dimensional system rather than from other planets or galaxies within our system is intriguing, and may better account for the facts. Although the general principle of relativity indicates that a spacecraft traveling at almost the speed of light would be able to traverse vast areas of the universe in a relatively short time, still it would not seem possible for these craft to return to their place of origin without experiencing enormous time differences. Thus, for instance, if an astronaut were to leave earth today and begin a circumnavigation of the known universe at speeds very close to that of light, he could undoubtedly accomplish this feat in less than 60 years of his lifetime aboard the spacecraft. But if after this time he contemplated returning to earth, he would find armageddon. By the time he would have returned the earth's sun would have undergone the last phases of its star-life, and the earth would undoubtedly have been reduced to no more than a glowing ember or pile of cinders in space. But if it is possible to pass through a warp to systems other than ours, systems outside of time, this problem would not exist. Would it not then seem much more likely that if, indeed, the earth has been visited by aliens in the past, that they have come not from different areas of space-time, but from other systems that may well be either contiguous or interfolded with ours?

We know all too well that our consciousness is almost totally locked into a four-dimensional system which we designate in terms of length, width, height and formally successive duration, time. Thus three of these dimensions are spatial and the fourth temporal. It is nigh impossible for us in any realistic way to conceive of anything outside of this system which holds our consciousness captive. We know what formally successive duration is because we experience how our life is payed out, second after second, minute after minute, day after day. We know also how the spatial dimensions are generated. Take a dot and move it in any direction and you produce a line. Here is the first of the spatial dimensions; designate it as you will. Then move the line at right angles to itself and you generate a plane. We now have the second dimension. Move the plane at right angles to itself and we have produced a three dimensional object, the kind we are most comfortable with. Is it possible to conceive of a fourth spatial dimension, and thus of a five dimensional world? Geometricians tell us that this is indeed possible, although it is hard for us to imagine the result of moving a cube at right angles to itself to generate the fourth spatial dimension. How can one move a cube at right angles? Where would it go? If it is done what is generated is a tesseract, a figure with four spatial dimensions. We move into the fifth dimension.

What does a tesseract look like? It is possible to represent in diagrammatic form in two dimensions, as on the page of a geometry book, a three-dimensional figure, like a cube. It will not, of course, be a perfect representation. Angles that are 90° become 45° angles. But we still can get some idea of the three-dimensional figure. Similarly with a change of angles it is possible to represent a tesseract in a three-dimensional system. Rendered in clear plastic it looks something like a smaller cube within a larger one. You might be able to find one among the paraphernalia of any high school geometry teacher.

Mathematicians like Lobachevsky, Riemann and Cantor have worked out the theoretical matrices for a universe of not merely four or even five dimensions, but one of n, or an indefinite number, of dimensions. For some time such machinations were deemed to be pure theory and in no way practical. But now, with the discovery of such naked singularities as black holes in the universe, scientists have come to realize that there have to be in fact the bases in the universe for other dimensional systems than the one we are familiar with. Light radiating out from a center forms one of the important measuring sticks in our system. It gives us the ultimate measure of the duration that we know as time; it enables us to envision the straight lines and angles which generate our spatial dimensions. But try to imagine a system where all things, even realities as lissome as a photon of light, move not centrifugally, but centripetally, that is, not out from a center, but toward a center. In the so-called black hole a neutron star exerts so much gravitational force that within the event horizon of the singularity nothing, not even as much as a photon of light, can escape. Were we to enter across the event horizon of such a system would we experience time as flowing backward rather than forward — would we encounter in miniature what it might be like if the whole universe were to go into another oscillatory phase and move back toward another big bang?

There is no doubt that Einstein considered c, the speed of light, to be the one absolute in the universe. But today there is some speculation among theoretical scientists about this. What if some reality could move at a speed greater than that of light? It would certainly lose one of its spatial dimensions, the one that lies at right angles to the direction in which it is traveling. Once the speed of light is exceeded, totally new dimensional possibilities emerge. The rules we have grown accustomed to in space-time no longer apply.

Thus it seems far from impossible, as a matter of fact, it may not even be unlikely, that in addition to the dimensional system of which we are directly conscious, the multifaceted fabric of matter can support many other systems totally different from ours, separated from ours by event horizons that we have not as yet been able fully to penetrate. We might imagine these as contiguous and co-extensive with our own, but all lying below the level of our present consciousness, like the bulk of an iceberg. Only when phenomena from these other systems occur on the event horizon between the two systems, or when they emerge from the other into our own system carrying with them alien properties, or more rarely, when someone from our system is suddenly thrust into another system and is able to return to recount their experience do we become vicariously aware of the possibility of such systems.

Space and time warps actually may not be just the gimmicks of science fiction. If there are other dimensional systems interwoven in the fabric of our own, and through a serendipitous quirk some of our people are thrust into them, they may well experience as present to them far-away places and other times. Some may disappear entirely from our system, and others may return to tell of their adventure.

Reportedly significant numbers of sea- and aircraft and the people they transported have suddenly disappeared while traveling in the notorious Bermuda Triangle off the coast of Florida. Some of the reports may have been spurious; honest mistakes may have been made; but still there are events that cannot be accounted for. An incident in point was reported on December 5, 1945. A flight of five torpedo bombers, fully equipped, left their Florida base on a routine training mission. Some time later a panicky radio message was received at the base from Flight 19, as it was designated, indicating that the squadron leader had lost all sense of direction. He radioed that he was not at all sure of his position. This was strange because all of the planes carried the standard navigational equipment which gave them more than one way of computing their location. Later reports stated that everything looked different — weird — that even the ocean did not appear to be normal. A short time later the base lost radio contact with the flight. Eventually a flying boat with a crew of 13 men was sent out to search for Flight 19, since by now it was presumed that it was in some kind of distress. Although it did not disappear without a trace in the Triangle, it, too, met with disaster: it blew up for no apparent reason at all. Later a large flotilla of search ships, some 100 planes and other land-based search vehicles were involved in trying to locate at least some debris from the ill-fated flight. Nothing was found.

Not only the disappearance without a trace of Flight 19, but also reports of other unusual phenomena prompted the navy to conduct a thorough sweep of the area of ocean known as the Bermuda Triangle. All sorts of sophisticated instruments were used in the search. But the investigation turned up absolutely nothing.

So the Bermuda Triangle remains to this day a mystery. Some have opined that it might be a space warp, an interface with another dimensional system, through which missing craft pass without trace in our world.

And it might have been that Anne Moberly and Eleanor Jourdain passed through a time warp when, in 1901, they were visiting Versailles, France. They set out on a walk toward the Petit Trianon, the lodge which King Louis XVI had built specially for Queen Marie Antoinette. They made a wrong turn on the path leading to the edifice and suddenly found themselves no longer in France of 1901, but rather in France on the eve of the Revolution in 1789. They recalled seeing men in small tricornered hats and long gray coats, women in antique dresses, and what might have been Marie Antoinette herself seated on the veranda of the Trianon. For a while the two ladies were reluctant to publish or even say anything about their strange adventure. But finally, in 1911, they authored a book pseudonymously. Only after careful historical research and the discovery of new maps of the terrain surrounding the Petit Trianon vindicated their allegations about what they had observed did they issue a third edition of their work under their real names in 1924. Some investigators of the phenomenon as well as the ladies themselves regarded it as some kind of psychic escapade, but today the possibility of passage through a time warp has to figure also among possible explanations for the experience of the Misses Moberly and Jourdain.

The data we have been considering thus far might

well provide a basis for a modern reassessment of the traditional theological doctrine about angels and devils. The first Russian cosmonaut, after exploring the space above the earth, came back and reported joyfully to his atheistic comrades in the Party that he had found none of the items that religion or superstition places there: no heaven, no angels, no God. Perhaps some naive people were taken aback by this great disclosure. Theologians, of course, knew better. But really they have done very little to inform us about where heaven, the angels and God might be located if not above the earth in the sky. Is it possible theologically to speculate that angels may indeed be what scientists call alien intelligences, inhabiting not some far-off planet or galaxy, but another dimensional system contiguous with the phenomena we observe on earth itself, interwoven with them, but not observable by us because of the limits of our consciousness? If they live just across the event horizon of our system, could they sometimes appear to us, communicate with us on their terms and carry out their God-appointed task of guarding us? And what about devils? Could they be in a different, but generally similar kind of system? Is not the search for creatures of an alien world fielded by researcher and theologian alike a most fruitful meeting ground for a profitable dialogue between science and religion?

Chapter VII

THE LAST THINGS

ASK a scientist what ultimately will happen to the earth, and he will undoubtedly tell you that eventually it will be consumed in fire. Our sun has been converting hydrogen into helium and, as a consequence, radiating massive amounts of energy out into space now for some five billion years. In about five billion more years it is expected that significant changes will appear in the operation of the solar factory. As the fuel supply in the sun's core becomes rarer and rarer, the core will no longer be able to support itself against the tremendous gravity of the outer layers and will begin to collapse. The interplay between the contracting core and the outer shell will, as time goes on, cause a great expansion. The outer regions will begin to explode and swell until the sun becomes about 100 times as large as it is today. It will become a red giant. It may continue to exist in this form for a few billion more years. It could then likely become a nebula, and finally pass through the stages of being a white dwarf and then a black dwarf as it cools off through billions and billions of years. The death knell for earth will sound when the sun begins to be a red giant. The increased size of the solar body and its mounting output of radiation will burn the earth into a cinder. Nothing could withstand the violent outburst of energy; the earth will be devastated in the solar wind.

We saw that some theologians today would leave it to science to tell us how the world began. Similarly some would say that it is really up to the scientist to tell us how the world will end. Eschatology, or the study of the last things, should cease to be a branch of theology. Such information as theology could have supplied has become effete in a scientific world.

But just as some theologians believe that the creation myth can supply a basic human psychological need, can offer an explanation for human existential *Angst,* many believe that eschatology alone can adequately symbolize man's undaunted hope for survival. Such eschatology would not be at loggerheads with science but would stand in an interface with it, complementing it and tailoring it to fit basic human needs.

The theologian considers eschatology to be the science of the end; it deals with end-time, of the final stages of man and the earth. He sees two distinct branches of eschatology, one dealing with the end of the world and of mankind in general, and the other related to the end of the life of the individual person. Usually when the term is used without qualification, however, it refers to the end of the world and of mankind in general. The traditional view of eschatology has related it to the big events in store for mankind: to spectacular and radical happenings that are yet to come. What will happen when the world is finished, when it comes to its end? Will Christ come as its judge? Will there be a general resurrection of all mankind? Will people be separated and those who are good enter into eternal life, while those who are evil go to eternal punishment? Will the earth in some way be renovated and become the habitat of the just? Are these the great events that people are waiting and hoping for?

The course of human history has evidenced a profound belief in the future reality of all of these events. And almost every era has had its prophets who have tried to predict when it would all come to pass. The followers of Joachim of Flora, for instance, predicted that the year 1266 would be the magic time when Christ would appear again. Joachim himself had envisioned three stages of human religious history. The first, lasting from the time of Abraham to that of Christ, was dominated by God the Father: it was the age of the great patriarchs. The second stage of religious history, lasting from the time of Jesus to that of St. Benedict, was the era of God the Son: it witnessed the model of the celibate clergy. The third period would last from the time of St. Benedict until the final consummation: it would be the era that experienced the reign of the Holy Spirit in the hearts of all believers — indeed, God's Spirit would become incarnate in the true believer, and his charisms would be manifest to the world. The followers of Joachim, encouraged by the religious revivals of the 13th century and the almost miraculous growth of the mendicant orders, predicted that the world would end in 1266 when Christ would come again to judge the living and the dead.

Since the time of Joachim there have been many prophets who have assayed to detail the time and events of end-time. Even today we hear voices raised in the warning that we do not have long to wait. But, barring a nuclear holocaust, the prediction of the scientist indicates that we still have five or six billion years to wait. Certainly the end of the world is not imminent.

Albert Schweitzer advocated a very traditional kind of eschatology. He viewed its events as a sudden and future breaking into the routine of human life of the kingdom of God. Until that great time of the Lord we have God's code of ethics to guide us; we are governed by a provisional ethic until the kingdom is established in power and glory with ultimate decisiveness.

Paul Tillich and Reinhold Niebuhr, on the other hand, advocate a symbolic eschatology. All eschatological considerations mean is that mankind cannot find its final destiny or full realization in this world. We are reminded by the symbolism that our goal is transhistorical. The be-all and end-all of our existence is not in history, but some other system. In history man must live in ethical ambiguity and insecurity until he reaches a stable state that is transhistorical. All of this is pointed up in the idea of a second coming of Jesus.

Paul Althaus considers eschatology from a teleological standpoint. He maintains that eschatology runs concurrently with history. Every generation dies and rises. Like the waves breaking continuously on the seashore, the believing community experiences a constant ebb and flow of dying and rising.

The noted British scripture scholar C. H. Dodd made what is likely the most significant contribution to the field when he proposed his idea of realized eschatology. Believers in early Christian times were looking for some kind of spectacular display in the sky which would signal end-time and the second coming of Christ. But God fooled them. The eschaton arrived and passed without their taking cognizance of it at all. For a while, even Paul was deceived. But eventually the Christian community began to appreciate what had actually happened. End-time occurred when Jesus died on the cross and rose from the dead. The death of Jesus marked the end of the old world, the world dominated by sin and ruled by law. The resurrection signaled the beginning of the new life, the reconstructed world, the world of freedom from law and guidance by the Holy Spirit. Rudolf Bultmann noted that eschatology is realized when people live in openness to the influence of God in their lives.

Other theologians, who like the idea of a realized eschatology and think that it indeed reflects what happened in the later writings of Paul and in some of the Gospels, do not want entirely to relinquish the idea of the eschaton as a future event. They feel that this notion is supported by Scripture too. So they propose what might aptly be described as an

inaugurated eschatology. That is, the eschatological events began in the past with the death and
resurrection of Jesus and the impact that this made
on the Christian community, but it has not yet been
completed: this will happen in the future when
there will be great signs in the sky — when Christ
will visit the earth again, this time with great power
and majesty.

Pierre Teilhard de Chardin, as already indicated,
sees eschatological events as simply the bringing to
its final conclusion in Christ of the process of
evolution that characterizes the development of
earth. His is a pancosmic eschatology, involving
not only human beings, but all the creatures of the
earth, recapitulated in humanity and especially in
the man, Christ. He projects that the world will
eventually be caught up in a marvelous transformation, which is indeed already under way but will
be consummated when world process reaches its
omega point.

How does traditional theology see this final
destiny of the world, its consummation at the time
of the second coming of Christ as affecting the individual? What was private before will now become
totally public; what befell the soul before will now
be shared by the body as well. The second coming
of Jesus will herald the resurrection of the bodies of
all, of the good to share in happiness, of the evil to
partake of punishment, and then will come the
general judgment or public commendation of the
good and condemnation of the evil by Jesus the
eschatological judge. But this will not change what

has already taken place. For the individual, shortly after his death, will have already been judged and his final lot decided. Thus for the individual, traditional theology has always proposed the four last things: death, judgment, heaven and hell.

The current theology of death has been profoundly influenced by the writings of philosophers, psychologists, physicians and researchers of all kinds. Most influential has been the thought of the German existentialist philosopher Martin Heidegger.

Heidegger relates the issue of death to the whole problem of evil. Death is the consummate evil, the greatest evil, for it implies the loss of absolutely everything. It generates the most profound of all fears and anxieties. Paradoxically enough, however, because it is essentially a future event, a "not-yet-for-the-time-being" it is also the source of all human hope as well as the courage to risk.

Because of death, time for man becomes the most important of the dimensions in which he lives. Without death there would be no marking of time, no counting the days, the minutes and the seconds. The psychologist Abraham Maslow concurs with Heidegger when he indicates that because man is under the threat of death, he lives and loves more intensely than he would if he did not have to die. If death can be thought of as beneficial in any way, this has to be one of the bonuses that it brings to human existence.

Inspired by Heidegger, writers have called our attention to the fact that death is symbolized in every change, in every separation, in every loss, in every diminution of a sense of security that human beings experience. Even before Heidegger, early psychological theorists have tried to establish a relationship between death or a death wish and the psychoses and neuroses that so often plague human life. We saw that the associate of Sigmund Freud, Otto Rank, proposed the idea of the birth trauma, that is, the experience of being separated from the total security that the human individual enjoys in the uterus and being thrust into a seemingly hostile world with which one can in no way cope, as the root of all psychological problems. The modern psychologist Rollo May looks to the other end of human existence for his explanation of the source of psychoses and neuroses. He advances the theory of the death trauma. Death involves the total loss of all security. Each of the great vicissitudes of life foreshadows death. There is death in every change, in every metamorphosis of our lives; we must let loose of the old, of the more comfortable, and embrace the new, the unknown.

Heidegger observes that death is such a unique human experience that about it alone we cannot philosophize: we can only speculate after projecting what it might be like — but, of course, we have no experience of it. While we really must believe in its facticity, we tend to act as if we are to live forever. It is the most personal of all experiences when it does occur. It marks the fullest possible growth of the human individual. This point especially has captured the imagination of recent theologians — but also Heidegger's notion that death is the final act of the human person. It is not just something that happens to him. It is a personal effort for which he must prepare himself. How reminiscent of old-fashioned preaching. For Heidegger, death is innermost. It affects the very roots of a person's being. Death is irrelative. It is the one absolute truth we have to believe in. There is nothing more certain than death. If one has no other belief at all, he must at least believe in his death. Death is invincible. No matter what is done, it is not possible to avoid death. It can be postponed, but not eliminated. Death will win any struggle eventually. This is one game that cannot be won. Losing in the games we play in life sets the stage for the reality, the ultimate reality that we shall experience in death. In the final analysis we all will be losers to death. Finally, death is universal. Everyone must die. Here lies a source of false comfort in the face of death.

Death produces dread and anxiety. Such anxiety forms a parameter of living that for the normal individual is most intimate and most influential in determining behavior. It affects the innermost areas of a person's psyche and being itself. The dread of death is the most absolute of all human dreads. It is the dread that, like death itself, is most certain to affect every human being and be an important factor in his or her development. This dread often has to be reduced in the individual by employing various mechanisms of avoidance; otherwise it would be too everwhelming and might induce a

paralysis or catatonia which would be psychologically crippling. A chief mechanism of avoidance is the rationalization which Heidegger calls
"one like many." It most effectively conceals the
horror of death. It allows one to flee from the
reality of death. It is based upon the fact that while
I am still alive my death can be known and anticipated only in the death of others. Death cannot be
so bad, because others have experienced it. Everyone dies. I can too. It is no big deal. I can be as
brave as others. But the reality of death for a
person who is realistic cannot be masked or repressed. For all it will pop up constantly in
disguised forms in the various vicissitudes of life.
Its symbols will be always with us. Every change
will foreshadow it; every loss will direct our attention toward it. It will deeply affect our behavior.
Many persons as they grow older become more and
more conservative, more afraid to take risks, as
they face more squarely the fact of their own death.

Heidegger notes that, despite its certainty, death
is indefinite for the individual as to its what, when
and how. Its facticity is thus obscurable. So it
generates the distinctively human passion of hope.
Hope rests on the persuasion that death is "not-yet-
for-the-time-being." But death is always expected.
Hope ultimately involves taking a risk; it is a
gamble.

The only realistic attitude that one can have
toward death, according to Heidegger, is one of acceptance. There is nothing else one can do about it.
So one must "run-forward-in-thought" toward

death. Here is where the philosopher's speculations and religious tradition coincide. For, in the Christian view, baptism is a running ahead in time to accept one's death. As we have seen, it is the celebration not only of Christ's redemptive death and resurrection, but of our own union with him in these actions: we herald our own death, the price we have to pay for sin, and our own rising to a new life in Christ.

For Heidegger, death is the ultimate reality principle that makes us truly human. Death strikes at the roots of the tendency we all have to self-apotheosis, self-divinization. Here, too, the philosopher makes an observation that is significant for the Christian. Death is the matrix holding the virtue of humility.

Death is also the ultimate reason why we should also be very much concerned with the now. Because we live under the threat of death, we must take advantage of what we can, when we can. We do not really know whether for us there will be a tomorrow.

The influential German theologian Dietrich Bonhöffer was executed by the Nazis at Flossenburg on April 9, 1945. During his imprisonment prior to his execution, he offered some reflections which have made their mark on the Christian philosophy and theology of death. He wanted once and for all to score the idea that any number of Christians cherish, namely that belief in the resurrection of Jesus and one's own personal resurrection is God's answer to the problem of death. He wanted to let his own witness and death point to a new kind of

Christian secularity, a new kind of Christian caring for the world, an anthropotropic theology of the present and the opportunities it offers. He wanted to demonstrate that our hope has really to be grounded in the present, in the now, in the current experience of life, not in the future life, not in things eschatological.

Bonhöffer makes a very telling point. He refers to the Church's firm advocacy of and belief in the future life. One of its essential teachings deals with resurrection. All of its doctrine has to be related to an eschatological hope. The orthopraxy stemming from its view of death, resurrection, hope, the relative value of the temporal as compared with the eternal and the certainty of God's promises, is personal mortification. Through mortification one dies to oneself in little things, to witness the fact that death itself has no hold on the one who believes. Christ has overcome death. The one who hopes in him and in the power of his resurrection is free from all dread of death. In baptismal initiation he has celebrated this belief publicly and sacramentally. He has embraced it with eagerness and joy as the doorway to a better life, life with God for all eternity. Yet the Church itself, the Church as institution, has not followed its own teaching. It does not believe. It is afraid to die to old forms of existence. It seeks its own security in traditional, tried and true ways. It will never admit its shortcomings and errors. It is not able to take any risks. So some of its members have sensed this contradiction between the Church's doctrine and its practice in regard to itself. If the Church is afraid, should not they, too, fear? If the Church does not believe in the power and protection of God, why should they? So their baptismal commitment is negated or nulli- · fied or compromised. Following the bad example of the Church, they, too, are afraid to die, to risk, to be humble, to mortify themselves. Bönhoffer reminds us that we no longer live in the age of martyrs. Yet in the ultimate analysis, baptism emerged as a substitute for martyrdom when the age of persecution was over.

More recently other theologians like Jürgen Moltmann and Wolfhart Pannenberg have recalled Christians to a more traditional kind of hope. Like Malraux, they view death as a transformation of life into destiny. They, to a certain extent, would side with the existentialist philosophers who would define man in terms of his future. Man is the only being who has a future.

Some existentialists, like Jean-Paul Sartre, are professed atheists. For them the question of an afterlife becomes meaningless. Yet, despite themselves, they have often, through their view of man, enkindled in others a new spark of hope. Their way of looking at man can be a source not only of belief in his possibilities, but also of hope for a better life in the future.

For the existentialist, human reality is situated reality. Man is not just one among the many *Seiende,* just a being, but *Dasein,* being-there, the being whose reality really lies in front of him, as a to-be-made. If man is not just to be, but to exist, he must continually transcend the present. For man the present never really is; it makes its presence known precisely by fleeing. Man lives in the future. So he must constantly hope. He has to learn how to hope. He becomes habituated to hope. So, even when faced with death, man hopes for something beyond. Hope transcends death.

For Jean-Paul Sartre, man's highest boast is his ability to choose. But even to choose is in a sense to die. For as Sartre points out, to choose is to annihilate the possibilities of one's being. If I choose to do one thing, I foreclose on myriad other opportunities. But, paradoxically enough, choice also opens up new possibilities for self-transcendence; otherwise we would not make any choices. So human choosing foreshadows and symbolizes death and the transcendent beyond. Man's essence as *Dasein* is achieved in every significant choice; but it is finally achieved, ultimately achieved in death, which is man's last choice. Man longs to be what he really is. But his essence cannot be fully captured until death; it always has to be hoped for, because it is never a fully present reality. Death is necessary to understand life as a process and to make that process a hopeful one. Could man make any progress at all if he were not under the sentence of death?

The Roman Catholic theologian Karl Rahner has also been influenced by existentialist thought. He sees death not as an impersonal happening, something thrust upon man from without, but as a truly personal and human event. This, he states, is not a new idea in theology. Both St. John Damascene and St. Thomas Aquinas recognized it. They emphasized the notion that death is not some kind of intrusion from without, but, at least in some circumstances, an act which man himself performs. They call dying a human act. Rahner writes that death is maturing self-realization. He sides with many other modern theologians and philosophers in calling it an achievement: it is the limit beyond which man cannot go in developing himself, in maturing. He discusses a problem raised by the teaching of St. Thomas Aquinas that the human soul, since in itself it is an incomplete substance, must always retain a transcendental relationship with some material reality. This has always been a source of difficulty for Thomistic theologians, since at death the soul is separated from its body. What matter then does it relate to? Rahner responds by saying that the separated soul assumes a transcendental relationship to matter in general, to all matter. Death involves a change from the particular to the universal, from one segment of matter to matter at large. Thus death actually expands the potential of the human soul to be immersed in matter and use it to know and to love. This, however, is not to be conceived of as if all matter were to become man's body. Nor does the individual soul become, as it were, a world soul. The soul does not become the form of all matter; matter merely serves as the ground of its being in a transcendental relationship: for its ability to survive as soul, and not as pure spirit. Death thus opens up the possibility of wider communication and a fuller grasp on reality without transforming in any way what is purely human into something angelic.

Ladislas Boros views death as man's final destiny and goal, and, as such, he considers it to be the determinant of every moment of earthly existence. The human will, he says, is not absolutely free; it is determined to choose what is perceived as simply good for the individual. In every free choice the will must always choose what appears as good. Now the total and complete good for man is God, but he lies hidden from man in his own world. Our intellectual grasp on the total existential good that is God is blocked by the fact that we have to draw the elements of our knowledge from material things. Only death can free us from this impediment. Perfect knowledge, perfect love and complete self-surrender are deterred by man's corporeity. All love has to be referred to the self in man's present condition because of the human person's bodily needs and demands. Aspirations for a truly selfless love can be realized only in the beyond where act can become state of being, decision can solidify into existence and time can be transformed into eternity. Death becomes man's first completely mature personal act.

Roger Troisfontaines seeks an explanation of death in the laws of personal growth. He observes that an individual can grow only through involvement and participation with others. Man cannot achieve personhood except in union with others. The individual grows in personal self-awareness through the community in which he finds himself. Without involvement, at least in a nuclear community, personal self-awareness is not attainable.

Troisfontaines uses the example of the infant in the uterus. The womb is absolutely necessary for the initial growth of the individual. It is a relating instrument; it permits the child to contact, in full measure for its capacities, a single other: its mother. Troisfontaines considers the human body to be another kind of uterus, a new and more adaptable uterus. It is the means the individual uses to contact the world and all it contains for continued growth and development. Birth is the first great significant step in personal maturation. When the infant reaches a certain stage of maturation, it outgrows the uterus; the uterus is no longer useful in sustaining its efforts at contact and communication. Thus it is also for the body. It is a law of nature that when a certain stage of development is reached, and the supporting structure can no longer afford the possibility of further development, it must be discarded and new modes of coping must emerge. When structures become counterproductive they must give way to new ones which will better serve evolutionary purposes.

In the uterus fully personal activity eventually is inhibited. The infant must begin to use its body to contact and relate with more "others" than its mother alone. But the further development and perfection and personality at one stage of the individual's growth can also be interfered with by the body itself, that body which up to this point served him so well. So death intervenes. The separation of death, like that from the uterus, is a radical one. But it is absolutely necessary for the attainment of the new goals which growth always demands. Troisfontaines indicates that people may live as infants, still clinging to the security they enjoyed as inhabitants of the uterus, but no one dies as an infant. In death each person achieves the fullness of his or her own personal psychological growth. Just as in the uterus a one-to-one relationship can no longer be sustained after a certain level of personal development is reached, and the infant necessarily, not by choice, is expelled from the womb so that he can contact many more persons, so when the fullness of growth that the body can bear is obtained, it is necessary to shuck off the body and to pass into other forms of existence where still greater numbers of contacts can be made and unlimited growth assayed.

What key ideas, then, are proposed by the current theological speculation on the important issue of death? First, that death is a personal act of the individual; it is not, at least for many, something that "just happens," but something that is ultimately chosen. Secondly, that death marks the full maturation of the human person: even if it is only an infant that dies, as we perceive it, it must be true that he, in the expansion he craves for living and growing, has to pass beyond merely earthly possibilities. Thirdly, that death forms a firm foundation for the distinctively human passion and uniquely Christian virtue of hope.

But basic hope, hope at least to survive death, is reflected also in the teachings of other great religions and the ideas of many thinkers who were not Christian. Consider the statement of Horace: *"Non omnis moriar"* (I shall not completely die), or Benjamin Franklin's, "A man is not completely alive until he is dead."

Key views on death supplied by today's theologians are already interfaced to a certain extent with the researches of such scientists as Dr. Elizabeth Kübler-Ross. Dr. Ross' famous study of the stages of dying in those persons who experience a gradual exit from this world is world-renowned. The first stage that she notes is that of disbelief. It is as if the dying person were saying: "No, it can't be I!" The second stage is that of anger. The patient asks the question: "Why should I have to die, and not someone who is less worthy or capable of living? It all seems so unjust! I am mad!" The third stage is characterized by bargaining: "If only I had done things differently! If I had given up smoking! Now I want to do what I did not in the past. If there is anyone 'up there,' is there any chance for me?"

The fourth stage is that of depression. There seems to be no hope left now at all. "Death is a certainty that I appreciate now at last. It is real; it really is going to happen." The fifth stage is acceptance. But then there is no alternative but to accept it. The sixth stage is that of choice. The patient is resigned to his fate: "I am ready; I will now to die." And then the patient usually dies.

In this particular concatenation of events it is

easy to observe the maturation that occurs in the very act of dying, a maturation that moves from stage to stage until finally it emerges in a first completely developed personal human choice.

Unlike the Japanese proverb, traditional Christian theology teaches that one can die only once. There can be no metempsychosis or transmigration of souls. On the contrary, segments of the Buddhist tradition hold that everyone has returned from death to live once again in the world. Under ordinary circumstances it is not possible to remember one's former life, but it is certain that one did live before. In fact, it is necessary for a person to continue to be reincarnated until he discovers the truth about the world and about himself. This enlightenment, or satori, consists simply in this: one must realize in the first instance that the world is an illusion; then ultimately one must come to accept the fact that even one's own self is an illusion. When this stage is reached it is then possible for one to be reabsorbed into the mind of the divinity and the curse of continual reincarnation will at last be ended.

The traditional Christian view that each individual can die only once, that each individual is allotted only one life in this world, has to come to terms with the findings of modern investigators. Under hypnosis certain persons have revealed in great detail and with seeming accuracy stories of their former lives. These accounts have been checked out by experts in history, geography and archeology and seem to be amazingly in accord with what is known. Some researchers have concluded that these reports are inexplicable if one does not admit that the person analyzed did indeed live in another era in another land. Here is an area of human experience where both science and theology will have to engage in further dialogue.

One of the more spectacular accounts of a former life is given by Dr. Arthur Guirdham, a British psychiatrist, who cared professionally for a woman patient who came to him seeking help because of the terrible nightmares she had been experiencing. For years she had dreamt of murder and massacre. With further questioning Dr. Guirdham discovered that this lady had written down a number of poems in medieval French when she was a young schoolgirl. Yet she took no courses in French and had never studied it. Certainly she could not have been in any way acquainted with the language as it was spoken in the Middle Ages. Upon checking further into her story about her dreams she revealed in them she seemed to be involved in a massacre of Cathars, who were 13th century heretics of the Manichaean variety who inhabited southern France in the area of Toulouse. She told of her own experience of being burned at the stake. She also revealed that in her former life, before her execution, she was kept prisoner in a certain church crypt. The psychiatrist himself investigated some of the details of her story. But he also secured the help of experts. All found her account to be remarkably accurate in every detail when they visited the sites in southern France where this woman claimed to have lived her former life.

The case of the return of Elijah the prophet, as related in the Bible, presents a challenge to the theological rejection of the doctrine of metempsychosis. Some people in Jesus' time believed that he was Elijah returned from the dead [Matthew 16/31]. Jesus himself referred to John the Baptist as Elijah [Matthew 11/14]. Some would say that this is only a metaphor, but others take it more seriously.

Another truth about death cherished by Christian theology is that it is a universal experience. Everyone must die. There are no exceptions to the rule. Even Jesus and his mother had to die, and they did not incur the guilt of original sin. Jesus, of course, did voluntarily assume the burden of the penalties for all of our sins. By his death he manifested that death is the penalty for sin. But the Old Testament seems to indicate that the prophet Elijah did not die; that is why it was expected that he would return. He was taken directly up to heaven in a fiery chariot without the intervention of death [4 Kings 2/1-11]. Scripture also testifies that Henoch was translated from this world so as not to see death [Genesis 5/24; Sirach 44/16]. The New Testament, too, commemorates this unusual event [Hebrews 11/5].

Mystery is not foreign to the theology of death: puzzling if not contradictory positions have to be sustained by those who see both the Scriptures and the teaching of the Church as *loca theologica* or sources for authentic theological information.

Roman Catholic teaching even today holds fast to the ideas that death can occur only once, that everyone has to die, that death is final and marks the definite end of earthly existence, and so finishes the time a person has for meriting or demeriting.

On the scientific side, too, there is considerable controversy about the whole issue of human death. Some of it centers on the book published by Dr. Raymond A. Moody, Jr. which is entitled *Life After Life*. Dr. Moody's book deals with the clinically dead, that is, those persons who give no vital signs, brain waves alone excepted. Eventually, through the ministrations of physicians or for other reasons, they are restored to life and are able to tell what it is like being "dead."

Of course, clinical death thus defined differs radically from theological death. As was indicated, the theologian would admit that a person is really dead when there is no natural possibility of his return to this life. The theologically dead do not tell of their experiences, unless one believes that they can be contacted in the other world through seances or the services of mediums.

What is remarkable about the tales of those who have experienced clinical death is how similar the details of what they underwent are. First, they agree that the full impact of the experience is basically inexpressible, ineffable. One simply does not have the words or the language to communicate what really happened. Many, as they were dying, heard their doctor or other persons around them announce the fact of their death. No pulse, no breathing were detected. A number of people in the over 100 cases that Dr. Moody studied felt that dying was not such a bad experience at all. They described extremely pleasant feelings and sensations that gripped them at the time of their passage. Even people who had been suffering terribly, who had been severely injured, felt a profound sense of peace and quiet. Many subjects reported that in their passage they heard a kind of buzzing or whirring sound. Some reported that they had the sensation of entering a dark tunnel or vortex after losing consciousness of their earthly surroundings. They seemed to move along at a good pace into this funnel-like apparition. Quite a number of those interviewed had out-of-the-body experiences in association with their clinical death. Some after a road accident reported watching — from outside their bodies — rescuers trying frantically to revive them. Others in hospital rooms observed emergency teams of doctors and nurses equipped with all sorts of paraphenalia attempting to resuscitate their inert bodies.

A considerable number of the interviewed reported having met, in their altered state of consciousness, friends and relatives who they knew were dead. Sometimes they encountered what they described as "spiritual beings" sent to ease their passage from life to death. Some patients described these spiritual beings in vivid ways; for others they seemed to be quite nebulous. Another phenomenon worth noting is a meeting with a so-called "being of light." This being of light was identified variously as an angel, as Christ, or as God or a god. The being of light was universally perceived as being benevolent, as reassuring and helping, as one whose presence was most enjoyable. Some others reported that as they entered the process of clinical death they began to review in rapid but vivid fashion, often in summary, significant events in their own lives. This review often was accomplished by means of visual images; at times it seemed to be provoked or aided by the presence of the being of light. A few of those who experienced clinical death described the happening in terms of approaching what might be called a border or horizon of some kind. Sometimes this took the form of a physical reality, like a body of water, a fence across a field, a gray mist or simply a line. Almost all of the people interviewed expressed the idea that they had the definite impression that they were given an option of either continuing the process of dying or returning to the earth. Some stated that, although they would much rather have stayed in the state they were in, because of special attachments, obligations or commitments to other persons in this world, they opted to return and resume their normal activites in this world.

Dr. Moody gives graphic descriptions of the experiences of a goodly number of the persons he interviewed. One of the conclusions that might be drawn from his analyses is that the experience radically changed their view of death. After their experience it seemed much less terrifying. And also the quality of their continued life in this world seemed to be improved by the experience.

Some students of the science of medicine are not impressed by Dr. Moody's accounts and reflections. They point out that what he described as the experiences of clinical death are really symptoms often associated with the phenomenon of anoxia, or lack of sufficient oxygen in key cells in the human brain. Sometimes even persons under ether, or other general anesthesia will respond in the same way: reviewing their life, entering a vortex, experiencing a great light, etc.

Another researcher, Dr. Elizabeth Kübler-Ross, looked for evidences in people on the verge of death or in those who experienced clinical death of a belief in the immortality of the human spirit. She herself seems to be convinced that there is indeed a life after death. But other scientists are more reluctant to admit that questions like this really belong to the scope of scientific investigation. They are more comfortable in leaving the issue of immortality in the hands of the philosopher and theologian. Empirical evidence seems to indicate that man dies like any other animal.

Some philosophers do propose and defend the thesis that the human life-principle is immortal. If the human soul is spiritual, then it must also *per se* be immortal. By a spiritual substance philosophers mean one that is radically independent of matter or its energies for its existence. It is true that in this life the human spirit does depend upon the body for its operation and activity. One cannot think without using his brain. But through logical argument these philosophers show that more is involved in human thinking than can be accounted for by the brain. Thought is itself a spiritual reality. Thus what produces it must also be spiritual. And a spiritual being does not have parts outside of parts; it is simple, and so cannot disintegrate or fall apart the way material reality does; so it has to be *per se* immortal. It will stay forever the way it is unless its creator annihilates it.

The first argument for the spirituality of the human soul rests on the fact that the human mind can reflect perfectly upon itself. This means that within itself the mind can produce an exact and perfect replica or image of the individual. This type of perfect reflection is not possible when dealing with matter. No replica of another material reality is exactly perfect: there are always flaws. Then, too, in material things the replica or reflection has to be outside of the reality that is imaged. It cannot totally encompass or be totally identified with the reality that is doing the reflecting. A mirror with its image is always separate from the thing imaged. On the other hand the human being by using his mind can produce within himself not only a reflection that is perfect, but one that is totally identified with him. Such a possibility, philosophers say, indicates the existence of a spiritual element in man.

Another argument revolves round the capability the human mind has of producing images of realities that are themselves totally immaterial. If I look at a house, the image of that house, reduced in size, rests on the retina of my eye; a second image is found in my other eye, and gives a slightly different perspective. These images are carried by nerve impulses to the visual area in the occipital lobe of my brain where once again some kind of image of the house, this time capable of three-dimensional interpretation, is reproduced. This image, as I perceive it, is extended in the same way that the house I am looking at is extended. Of course, in my mind, it is intentional; outside it is real. But otherwise it is exactly like the house I am looking at. The image fits it and it alone, not any other house, unless that too happens to be exactly like the one I am looking at. But if I think of what a house is, not of any particular house, I will produce two images: one material, very likely the image of a particular house I have seen, or at least a picture of the word "house," the other immaterial because it will be capable of fitting anything that is a house — it will encompass simultaneously all sorts of houses. It will be an image of the essence of a house, and that is a spiritual reality. When I inquire about that image questions like: "How big is it? How high is it? How many rooms does it have? What color is it? Where is its kitchen located? Is there a microwave oven?" are totally irrelevant, because I have not reproduced a picture of any particular house when I appreciate what a house is. The image I produce does not have any material qualities. It does not have any weight; it does not have any color; it does not occupy any space. In other words, it is a spiritual reality. And such a spiritual image must have been produced by a spiritual faculty in man: his soul. Similarly, if I think of what it means to be just, to give every person his or her due, I am thinking of something real, but which is in no way in itself material. Justice has no weight; it does not occupy space or time; it has no color, produces no sound, cannot be felt, tasted or smelled; it has no potential or identifiable vector; it cannot be identified as particle or wave.

In many passages the New Testament evidences the early Church's belief in a life after death. The recurring Greek phrase *"zoe aionios"* means unending or ageless life. The Gospel of John alone contains some 16 references. The earlier Gospels, too, are not without numerous allusions: Matthew 19/16; 19/29; 25/46; Mark 9/44; 10/17; 10/30; Luke 18/18; 18/30. Other New Testament writings demonstrate a similar adherence: Acts 13/46; 13/48; Romans 2/7; 5/21; 6/22; 6/23; Galatians 6/8; 1 Timothy 1/16; 6/12; Titus 1/2; 3/7, etc. The New Testament also speaks about eternal punishment [Matthew 25/46] or everlasting fire [Mathew 18/8; 25/41]. Mark refers to everlasting crime [3/29]. Luke speaks of everlasting dwellings [16/9] and 2 Thessalonians alludes to everlasting comfort [2/16]. So the early Christian looked upon death as a passage, passage to another world of everlasting happiness or punishment.

Some of the early Greek Fathers of the Church proposed an interesting doctrine in conjunction with this passage. It was the idea of *"telonia,"* check points on the road to the other world. The word *"telonion"* means tax station, or toll booth, sights that were very common on the roads of the ancient world. As people journeyed along they were often stopped and challenged as to whether they had paid their taxes. Theologically the idea referred to stations staffed by angels and devils in which challenges would be made to the wayfarer en route to eternal life. If he passed the challenges, he would reach heaven; if he did not he would wind up in hell or purgatory.

The doctrine of a judgment immediately after death, that is, before the general judgment at the end of the world, found its way into the conciliar pronouncements of the Church. Immediately after death a person is informed of his eternal status, and immediately after this the sentence is carried out: purgatory, heaven or hell. Some theologians speak of this judgment much in the manner of people interviewed by Dr. Moody: they think of it as a kind of summary review of one's life through which one comes to the conclusion as to whether or not he or she is deserving of heaven. Others refer to it simply as a kind of illumination of the mind to understand immediately what the decision of God is in regard to the life of the person: saved or damned. Of course, Roman Catholic theology holds that even if a person is saved, he or she may have to spend some time in purgatory to expiate the temporal punishment due to sin.

The teaching about eternal happiness or punishment implies that survival in the next life will be a personal one. The human individual is not absorbed into some kind of shared existence, much less into the being of the Deity, as in Hinduism. The Christian message has always insisted upon the continuation of one's distinctive personal identity in the future world. Most people would see no distinction between personal identitiy and individual identity. But as we saw, Pierre Teilhard de Chardin makes one. Persons will survive; individuals will not. In the hyperprosoponosphere individuality will have to be lost so that personality can make its last quantum leap into the area of shared consciousness. Personality for Teilhard is a relational reality. We can become persons and develop as persons only in relationship to others. Individuality, on the other hand, cuts us off from others; it separates us from our fellow-humans, and makes us stand by ourselves, alone, unattached, self-sufficient. Teilhard's idea might not be as incompatible with traditional theology as first it might appear. The Church has emphasized personal survival as one of its key doctrines, not necessarily survival of the individual as such.

While it would be of concern to the scientist whether or not human beings have a soul, the soul would not be the kind of reality science deals directly with. The scientist's primary function is to explore the mysteries of the material universe. But many scientists do admit that science itself, when functioning within the sphere of its primary competence, cannot either prove or disprove the existence of a spiritual reality in man. In its present state of development science is not even fully able to account for the phenomenon of human consciousness, much less for any spiritual element that might be involved in it.

Teilhard did establish a theory for the relating of matter and consciousness, attributing conscious activity to radial energy, as we saw. But he did this more as a philosopher of science than as a strictly empirical investigator. He wanted to put forth a hypothesis for discussion, not data for acceptance. The first step that the empirical scientist will have to take will be to correlate consciousness with various conditions or situations of neural tissue. This will be most difficult because consciousness is very hard to deal with empirically and objectively. Some theorists have opined that consciousness might somehow be connected with electromagnetic activity of the brain, with brain-waves. Others associate it with a critical mass of unattached neurons and their connections. But not much has been done to verify these ideas. Many feel that the task is impossible because the very essence of consciousness militates against any kind of purely mechanistic accounting for its existence. At best, they say, it can only be an epiphenomenon of matter. But if science at some time in the future is able to offer a plausible explanation for it as a phenomenon in animal life, and if investigations eventually can reveal something more substantial about the neural basis for the self-reflexive consciousness that is distinctively human, then the scientist will be in a much better position to dialogue with the theologian about what the latter has termed the soul or spirit of man. But we can certainly say right now that this spiritual element in humanity cannot function in this present life without energy supplied by the material element. Teilhard de Chardin put it very well when he said that we must eat to think. No one would deny that matter has its impact upon spirit. But the reverse is also true. There is hardly a physician who is not aware of the prevalence of what has been termed "psychosomatic disease," that is, true systemic, but usually functional, distress that has no known organic basis — whose origin, therefore, has to be attributed to psychological causes. A very wise physician once remarked that the stomach is the sounding board of the mind.

Some of the more unusual effects of the mind upon the body, as for instance the phenomenon of psychokinesis, cannot be satisfactorily accounted for even by today's sophisticated science. When the famous Israeli psychic, Uri Geller, by sheer force of spirit and without any physical contact with the object of his concentration bends forks and spoons, repairs broken watches, stops electronic instruments from functioning or raises sheets of paper up several inches off a table, science is at a definite loss fully to explain how these things can happen. Equally puzzling to the scientist is the so-called Kirilian aura that surrounds all living things when they are photographed using a special technique. Even once living things that have been dead for centuries show a faint glow in this process.

The theologian has assayed only the most general description of the various states or conditions in which the immortal spirit of a human being might find itself in the life that lies beyond this one.

He sees hell as one possibility. It is a place of punishment for those individuals who die in the state of serious sin. God's enemies are separated from him for all eternity. This separation is the very essence of hell and has been termed by the theologian the pain or penalty of loss *(poena damni)*. Since man's total orientation is toward the good, since his will can rest in nothing but the possession of what is totally good, hell has to be the most frustrating of punishments imaginable, the most extreme the human mind is capable of conceiving. The person in hell lives in endless remorse, anger, and hatred of God, himself and all others. In hell there can be no peace, no quiet, no hope — nothing but unending terrible frustration. The pain of loss is the punishment, theologians say, precisely for the turning away from God, the aversion to him, which every serious sin implies.

But in addition to the penalty of loss, hell also provides a pain or penalty of sense *(poena sensus)*. It is said to correspond to the pleasure or self-indulgence that the sinful act supplies. Scripture describes this penalty as fire, or a sensation of flames. The Bible indicates that this penalty, too, is permanent, everlasting, though some theologians in the past have opined that it might be mitigated or even removed as time goes on. They argue that although the affront to God involved in any sinful act is infinite and therefore deserves to be punished eternally, the self-indulgence involved in the act is not, and so requires only a temporal punishment. While the Church has never condemned this idea, it has rejected the doctrine of apocatastasis, or eventual full restoration and rehabilitation of the damned, an opinion dear to Origen and some of his followers. The position of the magisterium has always been that those who are condemned to hell can never be reformed or released.

Heaven is the place of everlasting happiness and joy. There human beings reach total fulfillment and come to possess, in God, the goal of their existence. Philosophers point out that the human will is capable of embracing unlimited good and the human mind is able to know all things. Only in God can these faculties attain fulfillment and perform perfectly what they were designed to do. Thus heaven becomes the place of supreme happiness and enjoyment. There one can behold and possess God in all his grandeur, glory and beauty.

Traditional theology is divided as to whether this complete fulfillment which human beings enjoy in heaven ultimately and formally arises from the fact that the intellect will behold God as he is in himself — will be granted the beatific vision, as it is called — or from the fact that the will completely encompasses God as the supreme good. There is no doubt that both of these features will be experienced in heaven; the only question is which one is the root and source of the total experience. The Franciscan school of theology, following John Duns Scotus,

holds that the possession of God as the supreme
good by the human will is the fundamental gift
bestowed upon the blessed. But, of course, the will
is a blind faculty: it can embrace as good only what
is presented to it as such by the intellect. The intellect also, then, is essential to the operation. But it
acts, as it were, like the handmaid of the will in the
process. The Thomistic school, the school which
has had much wider influence in the development
of theology, on the other hand, proposed that the
basic enjoyment of heaven emanates from seeing
God face to face, seeing him as he is in himself. For
these theologians heaven is formally constituted by
the beatific vision. The will is able to embrace God
as the supreme good only because the intellect ap-
prehends him as such in the beatific vision. Thus
the action of the will is, as it were, ancillary and
complementary to the operation of the intellect.

But how can man's finite intellect embrace the
infinite reality that God is? Theologians say that a
special aid called the "light of glory" *(lumen
gloriae)* will be given for the accomplishing of this
task. In heaven, grace will be replaced by the light
of glory as the basis of our participation in the life
of God. Of course, even with the *lumen gloriae* the
human mind will not be able to exhaust the infinite
being of the Godhead. But in the measure that one
has it, one will be able to appreciate God to the full
extent of one's capacity. One's mind will be filled,
as it were, with God, and there will be no veil, no
clouding of the image: God will be presented to the
mind as he is in himself; it is precisely this that pro-

duces the marvelous effect. The amount of the *lumen gloriae* that one enjoys in heaven depends upon the amount of grace one has at the moment of death. The more capacity for loving, the more grace one has, the greater the amount of *lumen gloriae* one will possess in heaven, and the greater the amount of *lumen gloriae* the more perfect will be the vision of God in heaven, and the fuller will be one's appreciation of him as the supreme good.

But the contemplation of God, though in the opinion of this school it constitutes the very essence of heaven, is not the only enjoyment the blessed have. There are extra benefits too. The person in heaven will also enjoy the company of the angels and saints. He or she will also be able to appreciate in fullest measure possible all created reality. Of course, all of this takes place in and through the beatific vision itself.

For some, the fact that people in heaven will be able to know what is going on back on earth presents a special problem. Will not the evil they see flourishing there diminish their enjoyment in the land of the blessed? Theologians say that bad events on earth will not disturb or lessen the pleasure of those enjoying the beatific vision because God's purpose in permitting these evils will be evident to them. They will be able to comprehend how God will eventually bring good and perhaps even better things out of what is apprehended as evil on earth.

Roman Catholic theology affirms belief in the existence of a third state, that of purgatory. Souls detained in purgatory are eventually destined for heaven. They have departed this life without the guilt of serious sin. But as we saw, there are two malices in sin: first, alienation from God, which is punishable by separation from God for all eternity in hell; secondly, self-indulgence, a preference of self over others which exceeds the bounds of propriety, and this is punishable by undergoing penalties that are temporary. The malice of self-indulgence can be expiated either on earth through acts of self-denial, prayer and penance or else in the future life by suffering in purgatory. In purgatory there is a temporary separation from God until the malice of self-indulgence can be atoned for, as well as some kind of sense pain which is also geared to make amends for the pleasure one has had in sinning. When the scales of justice are once again in balance, the soul passes from purgatory to heaven. At the end of the world, after all souls have expiated for their sins, purgatory will cease to exist and there will be only heaven and hell.

Those who are detained in purgatory can, according to Roman Catholic doctrine, be assisted by the prayers and sacrifices of people on earth. Indulgences attached to certain prayers and good works can be applied to souls in purgatory to reduce the time or extent of their suffering.

Roman Catholic theologians find some support for their belief in the existence of purgatory in Scripture. In the Second Book of Maccabees [12/32-46], Judas Maccabaeus orders a collection to be taken up so that those who have died in battle might be released from their sins by virtue of the sacrifices that will be secured through these offerings. What is implied is that the dead are being detained because of their sinfulness from whatever reward awaits them in the next life, and that sacrifices offered by people on earth have the potential of releasing them from whatever situation they are in. Again, we read in the Gospel of Matthew [12/32], that sins against the Holy Spirit will not be remitted either in this world or in the next. Thus the implication that sin can be remitted or forgiven even in the afterlife is supported by the text. The final reference made by Catholic theologians is from the first letter of Paul to the Corinthians [3/10, 15]. Paul here seems to be stating that if a person's works have been good, what he has done will last even through a purging fire, and eventually he can be sure that he will receive his reward; he will get what is coming to him because of the good he has accomplished. Some of what he has done may have to be burned, but he will be saved. If, however, he is saved this way, he will be saved "as one who has gone through fire." Obscure as the real meaning of this text is, it has been employed as an argument supporting the existence of purgatory.

The final state that we must consider is limbo. When one speaks of limbo, what is usually referred to is the limbo of infants, where the souls of infants who have died with only the guilt of original sin upon them spend eternity. But there was also a "limbo of the Fathers," where the souls of good people from the time of the creation of mankind until the completion of Christ's redemptive act were detained. After his death, Christ "descended into hell," that is, into this limbo of the Fathers, to bring them to heaven. From that time on this limbo ceased to exist, and there remains, according to some theologians, only the limbo of infants.

The existence of limbo has never been defined as a Catholic dogma. But it is defended by a large number of theologians. Since infants who die have the guilt of original sin upon them, they do have to be separated from God for all eternity: they can never attain their goal in life. This is true, because, as we have seen, original sin is a real sin, and its guilt personally affects every human being who is not baptized. But the second malice of sin, self-indulgence, is not encountered in the case of original sin. Thus, although there is eternal punishment — everlasting separation from God — in store for those who die with only its guilt upon them, there cannot be any temporal punishment, no pain of sense, no fire. So limbo has been considered as a place different from hell — although the really essential pain of hell, everlasting separation from God and failure to attain the goal of life *(poena damni)* as we have seen, is borne by those in limbo. Thus, for all practical purposes, limbo is really hell without sense pain.

Some theologians in the early history of the Church believed that those who died with only the guilt of original sin upon them went to hell; they did not conceive of such a place as the limbo of infants. But, since hell implies two penalties, loss and fire, these unfortunate souls did suffer sense pain also, though it was the slightest imaginable. Others thought that such an idea would impugn the justice of God. Such souls ought not experience any sense pain at all since they had never taken pleasure in their sin. They called the first group the *"tortores infantium"* (torturers of infants). They felt that there has to be a place where such souls are separated from God for all eternity but without any kind of sense pain. Thus arose the idea of a limbo of infants.

Roman Catholic theology has always held that there can be some kind of communication through prayer and the offering of good works among those who are in purgatory and on earth, and through prayer only in regard to those who are in heaven, in purgatory and on earth. This doctrine is termed the communion of the saints. It affirms a communality among those who are already saved and those who are called to be saved. The faithful on earth can pray to the saints in heaven and ask their help; in turn the saints can offer their assistance and succor to people on earth. The faithful can pray to and help the souls in purgatory; in turn, these souls can aid people on earth by their appeals to God. There is certainly some kind of communality between the souls in purgatory and those in heaven, although the relationship has never been clearly defined by theologians; it is not clear just how the blessed can, if indeed they can, give their help to the souls detained in purgatory. Despite the fond wishes of bereaved mothers who have lost their infants without having them baptized, this communion does not extend to those in limbo; really they are lost, not saved, nor can they ever be saved, so in no way can they be considered as saints.

As we saw, modern philosophy, psychology and science have significantly affected the current theology of death. Now death tends to be viewed as a kind of passage, as a maturing experience, as an act which a person, even though that person may seem — as far as his or her body is concerned — to be immature, must perform. This modern view, if it is accepted, has to exert a profound influence on the older notion of limbo, if not on purgatory itself. If some people experience life in this world only as infants, but if, on the other hand, no one dies as an infant, then the need for limbo is automatically removed. Limbo exists only for those who cannot perform as an adult and make adult choices. Once a person is able to choose, he or she can opt for God, and thus experience a baptism of desire, or to sin, to turn away from God, and thus commit a personal sin in addition to the original sin whose guilt they bear, and so indulge themselves that adequate punishment can be had only in hell. Limbo is not an option for an adult, that is, one who can choose: eventually for the adult there is only heaven and hell. Thus, if the act of dying becomes a choice for even an infant, if in the process of dying the infant has to mature to the extent that it can choose in a responsible way, and it has the option between God and sin, there is no such a place as limbo. The theologian and pastor no longer have to deal with it.

Protestant theologians often say that in the process of dying one is purged of any temporal punishment that may be due to sin. In this they would follow Martin Luther. But if such purgation takes place in the passage, then there is no need for purgatory either. Roman Catholics are leery of this solution, not only because of the pronouncements of the magisterium, but also because purgatory has traditionally been regarded as a state, a place, not merely as a subjective condition of the person who passes on into the next life.

As we contemplate these three different possibilities in the next life, purgatory, heaven and hell, we see that again science can be of great help. Could these conditions of the departed that belief has proposed be regarded simply as other dimensional systems? It was suggested in the previous chapter that what we call angels and devils might well be creatures inhabiting other dimensional systems adjacent to or interwoven with ours. Now could we say that hell is that system where both devils and damned human beings (demons) dwell? And could heaven be that system inhabited by both the angels and the elect? From a purely physical standpoint we do not know very much about those systems. But the theologian has already determined one of the parameters: eternity in those systems will replace time. Purgatory could constitute another dimensional system, but it does not have eternity as

one of its parameters. Rather it would have to have
a dimension similar to time, if theological conceptualizations of it are, even for symbols, rather
accurate.

What is most difficult for us to do is to visualize
a system without spatial dimensions. While we can
fantasize about unending or unlimited time, this is
harder to do in relation to space, particularly when
we know that the persons who have passed into the
other life must in some way be localized; it would
seem very unlikely that they would not only endure
forever, but also occupy infinite space. When we
think of the tesseract we see how difficult it is to
represent even one other spatial dimension: as we
said, how can one move a cube at right angles to
itself? Which way would it go? Science can only
assure us that indeed there can very well be other
dimensional systems, perhaps even highly complex
ones. But that is not of much help in assisting us to
visualize them.

We have considered end-time for the individual
from both a theological and scientific standpoint
and delineated some possible interaction. It remains now for us to take a look at the end of mankind in general. Traditional theology has proposed
this in terms of four symbolic events: the second
coming of the Lord, the general resurrection of the
dead, the great public judgment to be pronounced
on all mankind, and the possible renewal of the
earth to become the new habitat of the just.

The New Testament speaks frequently of the
great day of the Lord. The Gospel of Matthew, in

particular, emphasizes the parousia. Obviously the early Church was waiting in earnest for the return of Jesus in glory. He would descend to earth once again, this time in his resurrected body to call forth from their graves all of the deceased. Some of the Church Fathers and writers like Tertullian, Lactantius, Justin and Irenaeus took the text of the Book of Revelation [20/4-5] to mean that then the Lord would start a 1000-year-reign on earth with the elect. Nothing is said about what would happen to the condemned during this period. This notion of the reign of Christ for 1000 years at his second coming, known as millenarianism or chiliasm, excited many in early Christian times, and there was much speculation as to precisely when the great event was to begin. Chiliasm lost its popularity after the fifth century, but hopes were still high for the impending second coming or parousia. As the chain of events attendant upon this phenomenon gradually solidified in theology, the following scenario was eventually presented: the bodies of the deceased would first rise from the grave; all, both those to be chosen for heaven and the damned as well, would experience this resurrection of their bodies; the Lord's appearance in great glory would herald the calling together of all human beings, possessed once again of their bodies, for the general judgment. The decision about their eternal fate that was communicated to each individual secretly at death would now be broadcast for all humanity to hear. The just (with their bodies) would now be taken up to heaven, there to reign gloriously with Christ, while the damned (with their bodies) would be transported to eternal hellfire, to suffer under the hateful domination of the Prince of Darkness.

A number of Scripture passages reflect the notion that at the second coming of Christ the earth, and perhaps even the whole universe, will be renewed so that all creation will show forth the glory that is his and that is shared by those who will reign with him in the kingdom of God. Notable is the text of Romans [8/20-23]. Here Paul states that creation itself, like us humans, still retains the hope of being free from slavery to decadence in order to share with us the glory we have as children of God. A similar sentiment is expressed in 2 Peter [3/7-14]. The present sky and earth are destined to be enveloped with fire. The day of the Lord will come like a thief, and then with a roar the sky will vanish, and the elements will be bathed in flame and fall apart, and the earth and all it contains will be consumed. (Scripture seems here to catch a fleeting glimpse of the scientific prediction about the end of the world). But the letter goes on to offer some hope. It notes the promise of the Lord that there will be a new heaven and a new earth, a place where righteousness will be at home. When the sky dissolves in flames and the elements melt in the heat, all is not lost; the promise of renewal cannot be set aside. But one searches in vain both Scriptures and the writings of the early Church in general for a more detailed description of the refurbished earth. It is clear only that the cosmos which was once linked with mankind in sin and was to the human race a source of trial and tribulation will now be connected with the elect in glory and will be for them a fountainhead of happiness, joy and contentment.

One finds all the aspects of this final scenario for mankind save one anticipated in the individual's encounter with death: there is an encounter with Christ, the particular judgment and translation of the person to either a place of happiness or punishment. But traditional theology saves the resurrection of the body until the end time of the world. Until that time survival is for the soul only. The phenomenon of the resurrection of the body is, of course, of great interest to the scientist. How can there be such a thing?

Theologians have always taught that the resurrection of all human individuals has to be understood in the light of Christ's own resurrection. The Scriptures put forth Christ as the model of the resurrection. He is the first born from the dead. All the elect will rise as he rose. Although the condemned will also rise, presumably with the same kind of body that Christ had and the elect will have in the resurrection, they will not do so unto glory and enjoyment, but rather to be punished; their resurrected body will become for them an instrument of chastisement.

Sometimes people regard the resurrection as a kind of resuscitation of a corpse. I remember from the days when I was in grammar school how the nun who taught us religion described the phenomenon of the resurrection. She expatiated on how the various particles of dust, of bone and dessicated skin would all come together and form once again that very same body that I possessed on earth. Then my soul would return to the body and it would once again be alive — just the way it is now! Of course the class had some questions. If I die when I am 60 years old will my body look like it did then, or like it did when I was a basketball star at age 20, or will it look like it does now when I am 9 years old? With all the seriousness of a pope making an *ex cathedra* pronouncement Sister informed us that the body we would have in the resurrection would be like the one we had on earth when we were 33 years old. This is so because that was the age at which Christ died and rose. But what if I die before I reach 33? If I never am 33 how will God know what my body would look like at 33? Foolish questions! Did we not know that with God everything is possible.

Roma locuta, causa finita. But in every class there is always someone who does not hear or pay attention. What about a person who is cremated and his ashes scattered over the ocean? Every class, too, has its cynic. There are cannibals in New Guinea. What if a person is eaten by a cannibal? His body becomes part of the cannibal's body. Who will get what in the resurrection? How will God sort that one out?

There are multiple references in Scripture to resurrection. The resurrected do not marry [Matthew 22/30f; Mark 12/25; Luke 20/35]. After the resurrection of Jesus dead people began to appear in the city of Jerusalem [Matthew 27/53]. The virtuous will rise again and recompense will be made to them [Luke 14/14]. Those who do good will rise to life, while those who do evil will rise to condemnation [John 5/29]. Jesus praises Martha's faith in the resurrection, her belief in the fact that Jesus himself is the resurrection and the life, and that even the dead will live again if they believe in Jesus [John 11/24ff]. Paul expressed the belief that the reason he was on trial was that he hoped for the resurrection of the dead [Acts 23/6; 24/21]. Yet he holds firmly to the conviction that there will indeed be a resurrection of the good and bad alike [Acts 24/15]. He believes that we all will imitate Christ in his resurrection [Romans 6/5]. Paul devotes a large segment of his first letter to the Corinthians to the problem of those who deny that there can be such a thing as resurrection of the dead; he affirms that belief in the resurrection is essential for the Christian [15/12-42). He professes that all he wants to know is Christ and the power of his resurrection; he believes that by sharing in the sufferings of Christ and following the pattern of his death he can have a founded hope of taking his place in the resurrection of the dead [Philippians 3/11]. Two Timothy excoriates Hymenaeus and Philetus for claiming that the resurrection has already taken place. Hebrews calls attention to the essential doctrine of the resurrection of the dead [6/2], and mentions some of the great heroes of the past who came back to their wives through some kind of resurrection from the dead [11/35]. So there is ample testimony in early

Christian literature of a belief in the resurrection of the dead.

In treating of the resurrection Paul states very clearly that it does not consist merely in the resuscitation of a corpse. In I Corinthians he teaches that what is sown is perishable, but what is going to be raised up is imperishable; the thing that is sown is contemptible, but what is raised up will be glorious; it is something that is weak that is sown, but what is raised up is powerful; when that thing is sown it embodies the soul, but when it is raised up it embodies the spirit [15/42-44]. Theologians have warned that this passage does not mean that the body of the resurrected will somehow become spiritual. As St. Thomas Aquinas taught, it is impossible for matter to be converted into spirit. What it means is that the body will assume a brand new aspect, a condition or situation of being which is quite different from what it was before.

St. Thomas Aquinas gives a rather complete account of the situation of the resurrected body in the *Contra Gentiles* [c. 82-86]. First, he insists that the bodies of the resurrected will be immortal. They are no longer subject to dissolution; they are no longer corruptible. Secondly, he says that they will no longer need food, nor will they want sex. Of course, Jesus did not need food after his resurrection, but took it to show his disciples that it was not a ghost they saw, but Jesus himself in his resurrected flesh. He did eat, and therefore we can conclude that he could eat, even though he did not have to in his resurrected body. What about sex? I will let you draw your own conclusion. Certainly St. Thomas maintains that resurrected bodies retain their sexual qualities. Men do not become women, nor women men, nor do they become sexless individuals. The resurrected body will be impassible. It will no longer be subject to disease or pain. No one will be able to hurt it. Thirdly, the body of the resurrected will be glorified, that is, it will have a certain luminescence, a certain brilliance about it that will single it out as a body destined to exist in another world — in the case of the elect, in the glory of heaven, in the case of the damned (here is the exception to impassibility), to the non-consuming "spiritual fire" of hell. Fourthly, the resurrected bodies, in heaven will also enjoy agility, that is, the ability to respond immediately to the commands of the will. There will be no difficulties encountered in subjecting matter to spirit, no impediment in letting the body reflect the real desires of the spirit. These bodies, fifthly, will be subtle. They will be able to pass right through material objects like doors, walls and other obstacles. Finally, these bodies will be ageless; they will maintain always the vigor of youth.

Despite all of these qualities which mark them as quite dissimilar to earthly bodies as we know them, St. Thomas insists that resurrected bodies will be of the same nature as earthly bodies. He scores those who would say that the bodies of the resurrected will not have flesh and blood or any of the other humors that earthly bodies secrete. His reason for saying this is that he believed that the bodies of the risen would have to be conformed to the risen body of Christ. They must have the same kind of resurrected body that he had. Yet it is clear from Scripture that Christ did have a fleshly body, when, for instance as the Gospel of Luke indicates [24/39], he invited his disciples to touch and see so that they could witness the fact that he had flesh and bones, and therefore could not be just an apparition or ghost. Thus St. Thomas insists that the resurrected body must be in some way material, that it must be palpable and tangible. But of course the other qualities of the resurrected body — brightness, immortality, impassibility, agility and subtlety — preclude the possibility of concluding that it is exactly the same as it was before the resurrection. Again, we cannot emphasize the total identity of Christ's risen body with his crucified body. After the resurrection, Scripture avers, people, indeed his closest friends and intimates, often failed to recognize him; but all could give testimony that it was he who died on the cross — not even his bitterest enemies would claim that some one else than Jesus was put to death. The risen body has to be a transformed body, a different body from the passable, mortal, often deformed and unruly body that we bear in this life. The point that St. Thomas is making by insisting that the risen body is of the same nature as the earthly one is that the risen body is not a ghostly one; matter cannot be converted into spirit; Jesus possessed a real material body, though the matter may not be of exactly the same type of living substance that we are familiar with on earth.

How would St. Thomas have described the resurrected body if he had at his beck and call some of the particles that dance in the heads of modern physicists: quarks, neutrinos, photons, antimatter? Would such commodities have helped him to picture a body that is indeed material, and in no way spiritual, yet a body which could easily display those marvelous, seemingly other-worldly, attributes of immortality, brightness, clarity, impassibility, agility and subtlety, in a word, a body that is no longer destined to live on the earth as we know it, but in some other dimensional system of the universe?

In the consideration of theologians the guiding principle in regard to the resurrection of the dead is Christ's own resurrection. Bodies of the elect will be like Christ's own risen body. Now, if indeed the Shroud of Turin is the true burial cloth of Jesus, it could tell us quite a bit about a risen body. In 1978, for the first time in the history of the Shroud, a fairly extensive scientific examination was permitted. It offered strong evidence that the Shroud itself was not a fake. Someone at one time must have been buried in it. And whoever that was must have suffered in a way that was very similar to that which is reported about Jesus in the Scriptures. Even so, the odds are extremely high against its having been the burial cloth of anyone but Jesus. Scientists reported at the end of the study that the data substantiate two conclusions. First, the Shroud is an actual archeological artifact; in no sense, given all the circumstances attendant upon it, could it be a forgery. Secondly, it is very likely the burial cloth of Jesus of Nazareth.

The possibility of fakery in the case of the Shroud has been excluded by a careful search by experts in a number of fields for applied materials such as paint, dye, powders, acids and other chemicals. Examinations have been negative as to contact with any extraneous substance whatsoever, save for a human body. Micro-chemical analyses of the image itself have actually failed to reveal how it was formed. There is no known way today of producing a like effect with paints, stains, dyes or chemicals of various kinds.

One of the unusual features of the image is its three-dimensional characteristics. A second would be the extremely superficial nature of the image, which seems to preclude the application of any kind of liquid medium. Had a liquid been used with this type of material there would have had to be some penetration due to capillary action. Then again there are no evidences of brush strokes or of the use of an applicator. No paint or stain was used.

Some have proposed the theory that the image is a vaporgraph, that is, that it was created by the diffusion of gases from the body upward into the burial cloth. Possible sources such as sweat, ammonia, blood or spices have been proposed and rejected by the experts. They concluded that gas diffusion was simply not a possibility.

The simplest explanation for the image, some students have said, is that it was produced by contact with the body itself. But this notion too has to be discarded. In tests made with other bodies it was found that not all parts of the body which are definitely represented in the image of the Shroud could make actual contact in an experimental cloth of a similar nature. A much more active process than mere contact has to be postulated to explain the image of the Shroud. Moreover, the Shroud lacks saturation points or plateaus which would normally occur had the image been imprinted by contact with a body. Certain parts of the body, such as hair, would have left quite different kinds of impressions from those that are seen on the Shroud itself.

What alone would account for the unique impression on the Shroud? A number of highly specialized scientific tests were conducted to answer this question. Everything pointed to a sudden burst of high intensity energy such as might have been produced by a flash of light or heat and left a scorch-like impression on the surface of the cloth. As a result of the tests, this hypothesis was proposed, and seems to have been confirmed by spectographic studies made on the Shroud itself. These ranged from the infra-red, through the visible and x-ray, as well as the ultra-violet frequencies. The oxidation and dehydration characteristic of the image on the Shroud, the latent superficiality of the markings, the absence of plateaus or saturation points, the coloration — all point to a scorch-like phenomenon: an intense flash of radiant energy.

Scientists are convinced that the body that was in the Shroud disappeared suddenly, in a flash, in a burst of energy. This is corroborated by the fact that there is no evidence of the Shroud's having been unwrapped or unfolded in the earliest days to allow for the removal of the body. Had the body been removed by ordinary means, there would have been telltale marks in the cloth itself. Encrustations of blood would have been disturbed and other signs of distortion would have appeared. The only hypothesis which accords with the facts is that the body must have passed through the material of the Shroud in a burst of radiant energy.

But was the Shroud the burial cloth of Jesus? In the first place it seems highly improbable that any other human being would have suffered in exactly the same way that Jesus is described as having suffered in the Gospels. Moreover, certain data not given in the biblical accounts, but which modern historical research has uncovered, seem to be verified by the image in the Shroud. Thus for instance, that the ancient Romans crucified a person by driving a nail through his wrists rather than through his palms, was not well appreciated in the long history of Christian artistic representations of the crucifixion. Yet the Shroud reflects that fact. Putting together all of the details and facts as we know them from the Gospels and from historical and archeological investigation of Judean life in the time of Jesus, and comparing all of this with the evidence from the Shroud, one writer has estimated that the probabilities would be only one in 82,944,000 that the person buried in the Shroud was not Jesus.

The one scientific test needed for the final authentication of the Shroud of Turin as the burial cloth of Jesus that has still to be performed is carbon-14 dating. Those responsible for the care of the Shroud have been reluctant to permit any substantial piece of the material to be destroyed, as it would have to be in standard carbon-14 dating tests. It is rumored that a newer version of the test which uses a much smaller sample of the material might be allowed in the near future.

If we look upon the resurrection of Jesus as the passing of a body from our system across an event horizon into other dimensions, from the data provided by the Shroud of Turin we might conclude that the utilization and output of energy is quite different in the other system. Perhaps we could conclude that there is much less particulate matter in bodies in the other system, and that whatever solid matter exists there is more readily energized. Perhaps one could judge that in the other system energies do not seem to work against one another, that they are not found in counter-positions or so easily juxtaposed as they are in this system where we have to learn how to pit energy against energy to use the situation to our advantage. Could we say that the marvelous condition of immortality, clarity, impassibility, agility and subtlety can be achieved in the other system without the need for ingesting food to supply energy? If indeed the image on the Shroud is due to a burst of energy that is typical of bodies in the other world, might we say that that energy is quite different, and yet in some way similar, to that which we experience in this world?

But we must also consider that the risen body of Jesus, although basically outfitted to live in another dimensional system, had also to appear for some time on the event horizon of our system to give witness to the authenticity of his mission and teaching. If this is the case we might suspect that the risen body of Jesus had to have some of the characteristics of earthly bodies as we know them. For a while it had to be visible and palpable in our system. In order to witness the reality of the resurrection itself to a relatively primitive population it had to manifest qualities that are very much a part of our life. Although Jesus in his resurrected body did not have to eat and drink or allow his wounds to show, he did so in witness.

So there is quite a difference between the resurrection of Jesus and the resurrection of other people. The resurrection of Jesus had the added burden of appearing as a proof to a relatively simple people of the validity of Jesus' claims. It had to be a kind of spectacular, miraculous event, similar to those which Jesus performed during his lifetime. At this time, as to a certain extent even today, the principle of relativity could in no way be appreciated. So it was absolutely necessary for Jesus' body physically to disappear from our system. And this is what makes Jesus' resurrection unique. In the resurrection his body disappeared in a flash of energy from our system; the bodies of other risen people do not have to disappear.

So the Shroud of Turin may tell us something about the mode of that disappearance of the body of Jesus from the world. The tomb had to be empty if there was to be a witness of Jesus' resurrection in the early Church. How did he disappear? His body was simply disintegrated with a burst of radiant energy. His remains were annihilated or converted into a body suited for existence in the other system. The seemingly ridiculous search in the 19th century by Cardinal Louis Pie and conservative Catholics for the sacred foreskin of Jesus may indeed have had a point. That foreskin would have been the only substantial part of Jesus' body that remained in our system.

What if the corpse of Jesus had remained in our system after his death. Could people have believed in his resurrection? I think that in today's world there should have been no problem, since people should be able to appreciate that he simply assumed his other-dimensional body, that he continued to live in a new bodily way in the other system. But such a belief would have been totally unrealistic and utterly impossible in his day, so far removed from the principles of Einstein's physics.

A device that is often employed to distinguish various opinions about the exact nature of Jesus' resurrection is this: if a camera had been placed in the tomb at the time of the resurrection, what would it have recorded? Opinions range to both extremities, left and right. Rudolf Bultmann, who holds that the resurrection consists essentially in the rising of Jesus in the faith of the primitive Church, that his resurrection was in the psychological disposition of his followers, would undoubtedly have answered that nothing at all would have been recorded by the camera. Those on the extreme right would say that the camera would have recorded the resuscitation of a corpse: the return of color to Jesus' cheeks, the onset of measured breathing and the struggle to free himself from the burial shroud. I would hold that the camera simply recorded the disappearance of the body in a burst of radiant energy, if the film were sensitive enough to record both the infra-red and ultra-violet spectra. But I do not believe it would show that newly risen body of Jesus, the one he assumed for life in the other system unless he willed it to do so by appearing on the event horizon dividing our system from the other.

It is a matter of record that Jesus did appear a number of times on the event horizon between the two systems, once again, to give testimony or proof of his continued bodily existence in the other system. When beings from the other system appear on the event horizon between the two systems a person in our system does not have just a psychological awareness of that presence: physical disturbances are created in our system that betray the reality of the visitor. UFOs can be tracked by our radar. Photographs have been taken of what have been reported as UFOs. But from a scientific viewpoint, the impact of these aliens upon our system, the precise effects that they produce, has largely still to be explored. Photographs of alleged aliens and their spacecraft are hazy and undefined. One thinks of the lack of recognition of Jesus by his closest friends after his resurrection. Perhaps it would be safe to say, in returning to the camera analogy, that although it might have caught some image of the resurrected body of Jesus, its brilliance and clarity, its glory, its other-worldly aura might well have blurred or distorted the latent image of the film. At least there might well have been a considerable difference in the appearance of Jesus as left in the image on the Shroud of Turin and that in a photograph of him made during one of his post-resurrection appearances. One gives a view of his earthly body, the other of his risen body. One would have been a picture of him as people knew him during his day on earth, and the other a representation of him in his other-dimensional body manifesting itself on the event horizon of our system.

Authorities on the resurrection stories in the New Testament point out two items that must be considered as key elements in the accounts. The first is the phenomenon of the empty tomb, and the second is the fairly large number of reports of appearances of Jesus to his friends and admirers. While the second conjures up possibilities of illusion, hallucination or wishful thinking that might be associated with the disciples' feelings of guilt for having abandoned him in his hour of need or simply with some kind of faith frenzy that gripped the Jerusalem community at that period, the first, barring any fraud or chicanery, simply cannot be explained without resorting to some kind of very unusual happening or circumstance. The assertion of early believers that the tomb was indeed empty has never been seriously contested by the enemies of the Christian movement. The notion that the body was removed by Jesus' friends from the guarded tomb has at best been only weakly pushed. If it had been taken seriously, some one of the many adversaries of Christianity would have produced some substantial evidence to establish it as a definite fact.

Could it be that the resurrection of us all occurs in the process of dying? Is the following description plausible? As a person passes from this system across the event horizon into another one he is outfitted with a body, indeed his own, because it is his own vital energy that informs it, that will allow him to exist and function in that system. His remains on earth only evidence what was, not what is. Now he is embodied properly for a spaceless, timeless existence. Now he exists fully in another system.

And could this have been what happened to Jesus too, with the exception that his earthly body remained in the tomb for only three days before being consumed in a burst of energy, and his risen body hovered on the event horizon between the systems for 40 days? As we indicated, certainly Jesus' earthly body had to disappear so that his resurrection could be confirmed. But why wait for three days? Why did the appearances commence only after three days? Bible experts tell us that in salvation history "three days" has considerable significance. Jesus had predicted that as Jonah was in the belly of the sea creature for three days, so must the Son of Man remain in the heart of the earth for three days [Matthew 12/40]. There is evidence of a Jewish persuasion that a person is completely dead only after three days (recall it was on the fourth day that Jesus raised Lazarus; he was surely dead). Again in both the Old and New Testaments the third day seems to be the one on which critical, salvific action takes place. Joseph released his brothers from prison after three days [Genesis 42/18]. Yahweh waited for three days before concluding the covenant with his people [Exodus 19/11]. On the third day Esther finished her prayer, laid aside her penitential attire and began her negotiations with King Ahasuerus [5/1]. Jesus' parents sought him for three days and then found him in the Temple precincts [Luke 2/46]. Paul fasted for three days before being baptized [Acts 9/9], and so on.

Like three, forty is also a significant number in salvation history. Israel wandered for forty years in the desert before entering the promised land. Rain fell for forty days and nights in the time of Noah [Genesis 7/12]. It takes forty days to embalm the dead [Genesis 50/3]. Moses remained forty days and nights on the mountain of the Lord [Exodus 24/18]. While preparing to receive the law he spent 40 days and nights with Yahweh, neither eating nor drinking [Exodus 34/28]. Elijah walked for forty days and nights in the strength of the food he received from the angel [I Kings 19/8]. Jesus fasted in the desert forty days and nights [Matthew 4/2], and so on. So it was also that Jesus appeared to selected witnesses in his risen body for forty days.

Although Jesus' earthly body did, after three days, disappear from the tomb, bodies of the deceased today simply do not. They may remain for centuries in their burial places. This is the fact that seems to postulate that the general resurrection be a future event; it does not happen at the time of death as all can clearly see. If, however, we firmly believe that deceased persons do in some way enter eternity, that is, they enter into a different dimensional system of which time is no longer a parameter, then what is future for earth has to be now in that system. Not only does theology today fail to score the idea that resurrection is the resuscitation of a corpse, but also to let loose of time when dealing with the other system. As we said, in that system earth's past, present and future have to become a continuous now. How this can be may be a deep mystery, but we can come to some appreciation of it in today's world through a consideration of the general theory of relativity.

Imagine a person aboard a spacecraft traveling away from earth and continuously accelerating at 1 g per second (32 ft./sec./sec.). A spacecraft moving this way could eventually attain to a speed fairly close to that of light itself (Einstein's theory would never, of course, allow it to reach that exact speed). The craft would be able to circumnavigate the whole known universe in something less than 60 years. It would travel beyond our galaxy, ultimately to reach those galaxies known to us now only through the use of radio telescopes. The person aboard the spacecraft would age at the same rate as people on earth. The biological constants would remain the same. But while he passes through 30 or 40 years of his lifetime aboard the spacecraft, the earth relative to the spacecraft would be passing through billions of years of its existence. As was said before, when such a space traveler would return, he would find the earth charred and desolate, a burned-out cinder in space, and the sun just a thin veil of diffuse gas in space. At some point in the space journey, perhaps after 20 or 25 years, endtime would have reached earth. Since the spacecraft was accelerating and reaching a speed near to that of light, and moving away from the earth, time aboard the craft would have extended itself: time would have slowed down tremendously aboard the spacecraft relative to earth. If at some time in that journey we would consider both the space traveler and events on the earth simultaneously we might well see that earth was nearing its end while the space traveler was reaching the full vigor of his manhood. In a few years aboard his spacecraft the time traveler has been projected into the distant future of the earth. He has experienced how time is extended relative to earth for those who travel at speeds approaching that of light, and how time can be contracted once again at lower speeds.

So we might surmise that when a deceased person is being placed in his grave on earth his personal being has approached the speed of light; it is no longer in our space-time system; it is in an entirely new dimensional system of which time is definitely not one of the parameters. There is no question

here merely of expanded or contracted time: there
is no time whatsoever. Eternity is a perpetual
NOW. In a perpetual now there is no past and no
future. There the big bang and end time for earth
are experienced as present now. The case of the person aboard the spacecraft in our system helps us
understand the situation of the person who is outside time. But there is a big difference. The person
aboard the space ship is still radically in the time
dimension. He is almost out of it, but not quite. He
is almost on the event-horizon of some other
system, but has not quite made it. He is still in time,
and so can return to the space that he took off
from, but then of course he finds himself very
much in the future of that particular area of space.
He would not be able to experience the whole
history of that space, say that occupied by earth,
but only the area as it was when he left and as it will
be when he returns. Only if he can escape from
space-time entirely would he be able to witness the
whole history of any segment thereof. But this is
not to say that he would experience or, as it were,
live through all the events in a particular system. To
say that would imply the introduction of time into a
system where there is no time. We could imagine
that there will be a consciousness of these events as,
for instance, we can have an awareness of certain
areas of space-time that we have never visited, say
Africa, through television or motion pictures. We
know that on earth the dimensional system in
which we are immersed forms the matrix and basis
of our consciousness. There is a kind of reciprocity

between consciousness and dimensionality. Dimensionality delineates and defines consciousness, while consciousness creates dimensionality. When we try to become aware of a system other than ours, it might be possible for us to eliminate one or other parameter that we are familiar with, say time. But it is almost impossible to imagine a system with neither temporal nor spatial dimensionality. If we prescind from time we seem to have to retain at least the spatial dimensions. It would seem that in other systems our contact with matter would remain; that is why we would have a body. But just how and what aspects of matter that body would contact and how it would feed a new consciousness remain beyond our ken. At least theology assures us that there will be a new and more direct contact with God in the heaven system and through his own awareness our awareness of all other reality will be enhanced.

It is most important to note that, if indeed there are other systems in the universe supporting life and awareness largely unfamiliar to us, experience of that system is the exclusive prerogative of its denizens. There can be no experience dimension to dimension, although there can be consciousness of what is happening in other systems. One has to be situated in one dimension or another. One can never be, as far as experience is concerned, in more than one dimensional system. But this is not to say that one could not stand on the event horizon between two systems; but in that case, too, one would have to be situated essentially in one or other of those systems. Within each system some absolute predication of what is occurring in it is certainly possible, since this is the way everyone within the system perceives reality. Thus earthlings universally look to the future if they believe that there is a resurrection; people in another system might experience themselves as (pardon the temporal word, but it is hard to escape from one's system) *already* risen. The very dimensions of any system are in no way absolute, but relative to one another, so that where one may shrink or fade another will grow and expand. But all can be varied only up to a certain quantum limit which constitutes the absolute element of the system itself.

The idea of an absolute quantum limit is well known to scientists. Thus under certain conditions of atmospheric pressure I can heat water up to 212° F. or 100° C. It will just get hotter and hotter. Or I can cool it down to 32° F. or 0° C. and it will just get colder and colder. But at 212° F. it reaches its quantum limit, and must pass into another condition of existence in order to remain what it is; it becomes a gas. So too at 32° F. it must pass into another form of existence; it becomes a solid. Quantum limits such as these often are used to define the system. The absolute limit of our system, at least in Einstein's opinion, is c, the speed of light.

But what occurs in one system, even in its absolute quantum, can in no way be predicated in an absolute way of another system which constitutes or is constituted by a different and independent system. The one can be seen only as relative in respect to the other, and that relativity can support diametrically opposed events, system to system. The two systems can sustain a certain contiguity only along an event horizon common to both, but such an horizon constitutes an absolute barrier to event sharing in any common dimensional way. Events would have to occur in one system or the other, although there could be some consciousness of what is going on in the other system by persons situated in either one of them.

A practical illustration of all these rather abstruse principles is afforded by making reference to the Doppler effect, a phenomenon well-known to anyone who has taken a high-school science course. It is easier to understand when it is presented in terms of sound, but it is also valid in the consideration of light, which forms the matrix of our space-time system, and constitutes the basis of our consciousness.

Imagine yourself at a railroad crossing witnessing the passage of a train traveling at a very high rate of speed. You have several friends with you in the car. In addition, you are operating a tape recorder to pick up sounds at the crossing. All agree, and the recorder confirms the impression, that the pitch of the whistle of the train changed substantially as it approached and left the crossing. The possibility of a mass illusion is excluded by playing back the recording again and again. As the train approached your car the sound from the whistle seemed to rise in pitch and become shrill and penetrating. As the train receded the pitch dropped markedly. You and your friends could testify in a court of law, and confirm your allegations with the recording, that this is precisely what you heard.

Now in the cab of the locomotive of the train the engineer and fireman, whose recorder also confirms their impression, carefully observe that the pitch of the whistle did not change one whit as the train approached the crossing and passed beyond it. The whistle sounded to them as it always did — maintaining a continuously steady pitch. They could appear as witnesses against you in a court of law, and prove their contention by their own recording.

What we obviously have done here is to set up two mini-systems to show how, relative to a position in space-time, different true propositions can be predicated about the same phenomenon where some kind of motion is involved in the operation. In regard to the whistle on the speeding train both yours and the engineer's contentions are correct, even though they are contrary. You say: "The train's whistle changed substantially — very noticeably — as the train neared and then left the crossing; as the train approached the pitch of the whistle rose; as the train departed the pitch dropped." The engineer says: "The train's whistle did not change at all as the train went by the crossing; it remained steady as it always does." And both you and the engineer are right; what both of you say is true.

The explanation of the phenomenon is simple. As the train approaches you the sound waves from the whistle are squeezed together so that more pass your ear and the microphone of your recorder per unit time than if the train had been standing still. This is interpreted as a rise in pitch. As the train recedes from the crossing the distance between the crests of the sound waves is widened so that fewer hit your ear and the microphone per unit time. This is interpreted as a drop in pitch. On the other hand, on board the train its speed and vector do not affect the sound at all; so the whistle sounds as it would if the train were standing still. The riders on the train, relative to its whistle, are standing still.

Now the Doppler effect occurs not merely in the case of sound waves; it affects electromagnetic energy propagation as well. As was stated before, by reason of the so-called red shift in the spectrograph of distant stars scientists know that they are moving away from earth (which we fancy to be standing still like the auto at the railroad crossing), for red is at the low frequency end of the visible spectrum; thus it is known that we are in an expanding, or at least an expanding oscillatory phase, of the universe. Had the violet, or high frequency, end of the spectrum been widened, we would know that these far distant denizens of our system were hurtling toward us.

Let us take still another example. Each evening at a certain time of the year, we are able to gaze up into the sky and see a beautiful, bright star which, let us say, astronomers have named X 645 and which they contend is 10,000 light years away from earth. We look up at that star and say: "What a glorious star that is! It's a wonderful sight!'' But at that very instant, let us say, an intelligent creature who has eyes like ours and a brain like ours, but lives on planet M 893, a *Doppelgänger* of earth, situated 5000 light years closer to the star, between earth and the star, looks up into his sky and exclaims in his quaint language: "What a tragedy! It is certainly too bad that that beautiful star X 645 blew up in a great cosmic explosion several years ago. It was such a sight to behold! Now there is only a luminous cloud of dust in its place." If questioned, this alien would have to say the star no longer exists; and his statement would be perfectly true. But people on earth would have to say, if they could hear him and understand him: "Don't be absurd! Of course, the star still exists; we see it every night in all its splendor." Earthlings will have to wait about 5000 more years to witness the great cataclysm.

In these examples we have created, within our own dimensional system, two mini-systems to illustrate what does take place in a much more dramatic, expanded and spectacular way when we are dealing not with two mini-systems within the same space-time complex, but with two entirely different dimensional systems. If there is a possibility of verifying simultaneously two contrary propositions as true in those different mini-systems, then *a fortiori* that possibility exists when we are contemplating two systems with entirely different dimensional parameters.

So it is we on earth look upon a dead person as having lost his body, as being a disembodied spirit until the great day of the resurrection. We place his earthly remains in the grave, and hope that his spirit will rest in peace until the great Day of the Lord. On the other hand, the deceased person in another system will be at that very instant, as it were, already risen from the dead, will be witnessing, if he desires, the end of the world, the second coming of Jesus, the general judgment and (let's end on a happy note) will be enjoying his eternal state. Everything for him will be a NOW. Earth can see him only as a disembodied soul; heaven sees him as gloriously risen. And both perspectives are simultaneously true.

Only one question remains. Can theologians look upon eternity as eternity, that is, the parameter, or at least symbol, of another system, or will they continue to regard it as a kind of unending time, time that goes on forever?

Chapter VIII

THE CONSCIOUSNESS OF CHRIST

THERE is scarcely an area of theology today as replete with difficulties as that of Christology. But the central problem has to be that of considering a dual consciousness, human and divine, in Jesus. It is an issue that presents a challenge not only to the theologian but to the believing psychologist as well. All are well aware of the intimate connection between consciousness and personality. We are used to saying that where one encounters different consciousnesses there one finds different personalities and vice versa. While there certainly have been cases of multiple personalities, some human beings exhibiting as many as five or six different individuals, each seemingly unconscious of the others, there never has been a recorded case of a single person possessing two different consciousnesses at the same time. The closest approach is had in the commissurotomized person, but here there seems to be a division in perception more than in consciousness itself.

Modern psychological understandings of personality and the relationship of personality to consciousness lie behind the Christologist's problems with Jesus. Psychology would be hard pressed to explain how two consciousnesses, even if one is divine, can experientially fund a healthy person.

The Gospels are written in a quasi-narrative style as if presenting a biography or history of some events in Jesus' life. But of course we know them to be a kind of unique literary piece: a potpourri of history, Judaic tradition, folklore, hermeneutic, kerygma, parenesis, etc. It is difficult to sift out the historical from the other material. But modern researchers have succeeded in doing this as perhaps no scholars in the past have done. They have been assisted in this task by the recovery of hordes of ancient documents, like the Dead Sea scrolls, which allowed them to discover how the Aramaic language was spoken in times very close to those of Jesus, by the development of precise historical methodologies and criteria for discerning the historically spurious from the authentic, and by the computer, which is immensely helpful in doing the kind of searching required, for instance, in reconstructing the speech patterns of Jesus. One result of this painstaking research has been to suggest that Jesus' sayings were remembered for so long a time because he spoke not in prose, but in poetic form: an Aramaic couplet or double couplet with a four beat rythm in the stichs, with a great deal of alliteration (he seemed to be fond of m and n sounds), with assonant rhyme and a sharp contrast of images in his presentations.

So modern scholarship has focused more upon the humanity of Jesus, and has played down his divinity. And this seems to be much in accord with the penchant, particularly of young people today (evidenced perhaps in the musicals *Jesus Christ*

Superstar and *Godspell* as well as in the literature of the time), to learn more about Jesus the man. So there has emerged, especially today, a Christology "from below," that is, one which begins with the humanity of Jesus and concentrates on his human activity, as over against the older Christology "from above," or one which emphasizes the faith position that Jesus is a divine person, and evaluates and appreciates all of the human activity of Jesus in the light of this presupposition. A Christology from below has to rely very much upon psychological data in order to understand what went on in Jesus' human life. Psychology is certainly a much less demanding science than, say, physics. It is itself sufficiently humanistic to be appreciated by those who have largely a humanistic background and little training in the exact sciences. And it is this science that has introduced a snag into the hitherto harmonized and unchallenged theological construct about the consciousness of Jesus. Psychology poses the problem, but really cannot offer a solution. Nor does philosophy offer much help. But it is possible that the general theory of relativity would be an avenue to explore in acculturating our belief that Jesus was indeed a divine person with both a divine and human nature and the distinctive awarenesses of each of those natures. Relativity is always a perilous area, and we approach an application of it to the issue of Jesus' real humanity only with a great deal of tentativeness. But we think a look at the possibilities it does offer may stimulate theologians and others to reflect more on this knotty problem of Christology.

Traditional theology defends the doctrine that Jesus is indeed the Son of God. He is the Logos, the Second Person of the Trinity, the perfect image of the Father, generated by him and sharing with him and the Spirit the divine nature for all eternity. But Jesus Christ, that divine Logos, is also a human being, the son of Mary, generated by her and sharing with her and all people a human nature in time. This is the mystery of the Incarnation.

As the doctrine developed historically many difficulties and problems have surfaced. Judaism denied the divinity of Jesus right from the beginning, and most Jews have also refused to acknowledge Jesus' claims to Messiahship. The notion that a divine being could in any real sense become incarnated in human flesh has always been repugnant to rationalist philosophers. The Docetists in the early Church would not acknowledge that Jesus' human body was a real one. They maintained that indeed he was divine, but his human body was an illusion: he appeared to be human in order to deal with human beings. Arius, on the other hand, taught that the divine Logos united himself with real flesh. But he had no human spirit, no soul. The Logos, as it were, took the place of a human soul in Jesus' flesh. Apollinaris affirmed that Jesus possessed both a human spirit and flesh; what he lacked was a human ability to reason, a human consciousness; his consciousness, the only one he possessed, was

divine. The condemnation in the early history of
the Church of this error puts theologians today in
the position of having to affirm two intellectual
faculties and two awarenesses in Jesus.

Nestorius proposed the idea that there were in
Jesus two different persons, one human and the
other divine. Between them there was an intimate
union; Nestorius said that the Son of God dwelled
in Jesus the man as in a temple. The Council of
Chalcedon condemned this notion, and eventually
there emerged the position that the two natures in
Christ were united in his divine personhood: the
dogma of the hypostatic union. By nature theologians understand the being of a reality considered
as a total operational faculty. It is in virtue of my
human nature that I perform human actions, that I
operate on a human level, in a human sphere,
humanly. Thus the Council of Chalcedon affirmed
that the person Jesus, identified with the divine
Logos, was able to operate both on the divine level
as God, and on a human level as true man.

The theologian has quite a different notion of the
person from that of the psychologist. Many psychologists themselves have great difficulty in defin-
ing just what constitutes personality. Often their
definition will be made in reference to characteristic behavior patterns, typical ways of evaluating
and acting attributed to the an individual. On the
other hand, the theologian's definition of personhood is quite simple; he sees it as the ultimate subject of responsibility. It is the answer to the question: "Who did it? Who is responsible?" It is

always the person who acts, the person who is responsible. So in Jesus, theologians say, we find only one subject of responsibility: it is the Logos or Second Person of the Trinity. He is ultimately the responsible agent for all activities that are attributable to either of his two natures or both of them combined. Thus if he weeps, it is the Logos who weeps; if he raises Lazarus from the dead, it is the Logos whose power is manifest.

Eutyches of Constantinople is looked upon as the founder of the heresy known as monophysitism. It teaches that both the divine and human activities of Jesus emanate from a single principle of operation — not from a single person — that is, a single, combined nature, a new creation that evidences both human and divine qualities. Sergius of Constantinople rejected monophysitism, but espoused monothelitism: the doctrine that proposes that, although there really are two distinct natures in Christ, there is only one will and one operation. The activities of the two natures are, as it were, amalgamated into one single flow of energy. Against Eutyches Church councils have defined that there is not confusion of the two distinct natures in Christ. There have to be two different substances, one divine and the other human. Each substance is complete in itself, and there is no comingling or mixture of the two. Against Sergius authoritative bodies in the Church have defined that there are two separate wills in Christ, one divine and the other human, as well as two operations, one divine and the other human. Theologians have maintained, however, that these two wills and two operations work in perfect unity and harmony with each other. So they have advanced the idea of a theandric (God-man) operation. This means that the activity emanating from the two distinct natures is so complementary and coordinated that it might seem to flow from a single nature, but, of course, it really does not since it maintains a relationship either to the divine or human faculties involved. Sometimes, however, it is possible to designate the nature principally or exclusively involved, as in the working of miracles, the uttering of prophecies, eating, sleeping, experiencing pain. But it is not merely the activities that are so tightly connected. Theologians have always affirmed that the natures themselves in the hypostatic union are inseparable and intimately united, though always distinguishable. They invented the special term *perichoresis* fully to express the perfect harmony and interpenetration of the two natures in the single person of the Logos. Perichoresis designates the perfect mutual in-existence of the two natures. The use of the term "in-existence" however does not preclude the possibility of theologians' debating whether there are in Christ two distinct existences, one divine and the other human, or both are united in one existence. While ecclesiastical teaching has emphasized the distinction between the natures and operations in Christ, the issue of whether there are two distinct existences or only one has never been definitely settled.

Theologians speak about a "communication of

idioms" in conjunction with the doctrine of the incarnation. This device has profoundly affected the devotional life of Christians. We take it for granted so often when offering our prayers. Strictly speaking, what it involves is a theological error; but because it is a way of speaking that tradition has allowed, it can be employed freely. In communicating idioms the theologian transfers properties of one nature to the other; this may be done because of the unity or perichoresis of the two natures in the single divine person. So human actions of Jesus may be attributed to the divine nature, and conversely, divine actions to the human nature, because really there is only one subject of responsibility linking the two natures together in an inseparable bond. Thus by reason of the communication of idioms it is correct to say that God suffered and that Mary is the mother of God. When specifying a nature, however, one must be wary. It is not proper to say that Christ as man created the world, or that Jesus as God was crucified. On the other hand, it would be correct to say that the man Jesus is the real Son of God. In the past many disputes and arguments have arisen among theologians about the proper use of the communication of idioms. A number of usages have specifically been called into question. Can we say that Christ is the servant of God (when really he is the Son of God)? Is it erroneous to preach that one of the Trinity was crucified? Surely both of these propositions could be understood in an orthodox sense, and there would be no problem at all about using them with a fairly sophisticated audience. On the other hand, the proposition that the man Jesus is present everywhere, as it is found in Lutheran spiritual doctrine, might well be suspect. The gnostic Gospel of Thomas has a similar idea [log. 77]: "Jesus said . . . : Cleave the wood and you will find me; lift up the stone and I am there."

Much has been written about the knowledge of Jesus. Of course, as a divine person he enjoys the infinite knowledge of God himself. Theologians have taught that in his humanity, from the first moment of his existence, Jesus also basked in the beatific vision, the knowledge of the blessed in heaven. In addition to this, they aver that he revels in infused knowledge. In other words, he has the same kind of knowledge as the angelic host possesses without any expenditure of energy or requirement for study. Finally theologians attribute to the human nature of Jesus experiential knowledge, the kind of knowledge that all of us have as human beings — only Jesus possessed it in an uncommon way, like the most intelligent of earthlings. Thus Jesus, according to the traditional theology seems to have a literal glut of knowledge.

When Scripture indicates that Jesus progressed in knowledge, theologians say that it is obvious that reference is made to his experiential knowledge. It alone can grow and be perfected. Experiential knowledge begins in sense perception and culminates in the use of reason. As we said, many theologians, following St. Thomas Aquinas, hold that even the experiential knowledge of Christ, at the time his manhood was flourishing, must have approached perfection, at least to the extent that his knowledge was more perfect than any other creature of the same order. Otherwise, St. Thomas says, Christ could not be considered the head of all creation. If his infused knowledge was more perfect than that of any angel, and if his experiential knowledge outstripped that of any other human, then alone could he attain that dominance over all creation that Scripture attests is his right.

But theologians also teach that Jesus, in his humanity, endowed with the beatific vision as it was, still did not fully comprehend God, since the human intellect always remains finite, while the being of God is infinite, and it is absolutely impossible to place an infinite reality, in any experiential way, in a finite faculty. So even in the beatific vision which he possessed from the beginning of his human existence Jesus saw God in only a limited way, even though it was a highly perfect grasp that he had of God, more perfect than that of any of the blessed in heaven. Like the blessed, Christ saw God face to face during his earthly life, but always in a human way, in accordance with his human capacity to know. Like the just in heaven, he possessed the light of glory *(lumen gloriae);* through it he enjoyed the beatific vision on earth.

Theologians surmise that through the beatific vision and infused knowledge that he enjoyed, if not in his experiential knowledge, Jesus must have been aware from the beginning that he was God, and that he had a messianic calling. The doctrine of the

Modernists that Christ did not always possess the consciousness of his messianic vocation has been condemned. But it is not likely that these theological understandings should be referred to the experiential knowledge of Jesus. Here he had to grow in self-awareness and awareness of the world around him just as anyone else does.

Why did Jesus need so much knowledge? As we said, he seemed to be over-supplied with knowledge, to be glutted with it. Would it not have been sufficient for him and still complicated enough for theology if he had just two kinds of knowledge, divine and experiential? Could we employ Ockham's razor: *"Entia non sunt multiplicanda sine ratione"* (Entities ought not to be multiplied without reason)? If he had divine knowledge, would not this have placed him ahead of any creature? And in it would he not have possessed at least eminently any creaturely knowledge? The medieval theologians seemed to be taken by a spirit of overkill in this matter of knowledge.

Along parallel lines an argument was mounted in regard to the body of Jesus. It had to be the most perfect of any human being. He was not liable to any defects or disease. He was incapable of any suffering arising from internal causes. With his permission he could suffer — as he did on the cross — when injury was inflicted from without.

More recently, theologians tend to pass over this supposition that Jesus had to be the absolutely most perfect creation of God — at least before his resurrection. The person of today tends to respond more fully, authentically and appreciatively to a Christ who was a genuine human being without needing to have him be the most perfect human being. He could be the greatest for them even if he did not have angelic infused knowledge or the beatific vision; in fact, many would admire him more if he did not. Nor did he have to have a body immune from disease and disorder; the more he is like us, the more genuinely human he is, the more significant is his soteriological message for the person in the street today.

If we can believe that the Shroud of Turin is the burial cloth of Jesus, we may have some evidence that his body was not indeed free of all disease. He could have been a victim of Marfan's syndrome. The image of the Shroud is dolichocephalic (characterized by a long thin head); the bone structure in general reveals a long, thin frame; the hands are abnormally large; the eyes are deep-set. Marfan's syndrome is a disorder of the connective tissue involving defects in the aortic arch and leading to a premature death. If Jesus had not been crucified, it would have been unlikely that he would have lived much longer anyway. It is not clear from the image on the Shroud whether this would be the case with Jesus or not, but another problem often associated with Marfan's syndrome is *ectopia lentis* (misplacement of the lens of the eye). But the general symptoms of the syndrome discernible from the bodily frame are pretty much in evidence in the image on the Shroud.

People always ask how Jesus could have suffered

so terribly if he was experiencing the beatific vision during the time of his passion. There has to be a problem here. Either the beatific vision is not what it is cracked up to be, or else Jesus went through the externals of the passion but really felt no pain — quite the contrary: his body was suffused with the incredible joy and pleasure that the risen blessed enjoy in heaven. Of course one answer to this dilemma might be that Jesus did not at the time of his passion have the same kind of a body that the risen blessed have; as we saw in the last chapter, if you accept the idea that the risen body is one outfitted for life in the other world, then it has to be impassible; but Jesus at the time of his passion had a real earthly body, one quite capable of suffering. But even so, we imagine that one who possesses God in such a radical way as one would in the beatific vision would be filled with an exhilaration that is beyond our wildest projections and be entirely insensitive to pain, even the terrible pain of the crucifixion. If even hypnosis can free us from pain, I would suspect that the beatific vision would, too. How could one with the beatific vision in any real sense quote Psalm 22/1: "My God, my God, why have you forsaken me?" [Cf. Matthew 27/46].

Or if Jesus had angelic knowledge, infused knowledge, would he have not known who touched him when power went out from him to heal the woman suffering from a hemorrhage [Mark 5/30-33]? Or what about the mistakes that have to be attributed either to Jesus himself or to those who composed the Gospels or copied the manuscripts?

It was Ahimelech and not Abiathar who was high priest at the time that David and his men went into the house of God and ate the loaves of offering that only the priests were allowed to eat [Mark 2/26; I Samuel 21/ 1-6]. There is an error in identifying the Zechariah who was murdered in the temple between the sanctuary and the altar. It was Zechariah the son of Jehoiada, not the Zechariah who was the son of Barachiah as Jesus says in the Gospel [Matthew 23/35; 2 Chronicles 24/20-22]. Then again, Psalm 110 is neither a psalm of David nor a messianic psalm as Jesus thought [Mark 12/36]. Would not anyone, even in Jesus' time, have known that if a seed in the ground dies, it does not produce a plant — only a seed that stays alive germinates [John 12/24]? Jesus predicted that in the destruction that would come upon Jerusalem there would not be in the Temple a stone left upon a stone [Mark 13/2]. Yet the Roman soldiers kept a part of the Temple mound for their camp, and so we have the wailing wall even today. It would not take infused knowledge, but just ordinary observation to know that the mustard seed does not grow into a magnificent tree, but just a scrubby bush [Matthew 13/32; Mark 4/31; Luke 13/19].

Indeed are there any indications in the New Testament that before his resurrection Jesus did not have divine knowledge? If he had the self-consciousness of God how could he say that the Father is greater than he [John 14/28]. Did he not know that he and the Father are equal? If one would say that this refers to his human nature alone, then we have to worry about the validity of the communication of idioms. Or why did he warn his followers not to call him good, because only one is good, namely God [Mark 10/18]? More particularly why would he say that the time of the final consummation of the world is not known to the angels nor to himself, but to the Father alone [Matthew 24/36; Mark 13/32]? Should he not have said that he knew it, but could not reveal it? Then, too, was he not mistaken in his notion that end-time was imminent? Is there a contradiction in Jesus' teaching that the flesh profits nothing [John 6/63] and then warning that one must eat his flesh in order to have life in him [John 6/53]? Or is there a distinction between flesh and flesh?

There is no doubt that there are many indications in the Gospel that Jesus knew the hidden and secret thoughts of other people. He also seemed to have known some events that were occurring or had occurred at a distance when it did not seem that he could have obtained that knowledge by ordinary means. But do we not run into a similar phenomenon today? Are there not psychics, or at least people sensitive enough, to know the hidden thoughts of others and to pick up information about events that are occurring at a distance?

The issue of the knowledge of Jesus is, of course, closely connected with that of his consciousness. Consciousness is intimately connected not only with nature (I have a human consciousness because I am a human being) but also with personhood (my consciousness is distinctively mine: it is the way I perceive that I am I and not someone else). If we are tempted to say that because Jesus possessed two distinct natures, one divine and the other human, he also was endowed with two consciousnesses, one divine and the other human, we run afoul of a perplexing psychological puzzle. How could Jesus then be a real person? If personality designates only a hook on which to hang actions, if it means only an ultimate subject of responsibility as it did for the medieval theologians, then there is not much of a problem. The one who was responsible for all of Jesus' actions, whether they flowed from the divine or the human nature, is the Logos, the Son of God. But if, as modern psychologists opine, personality indicates a unified center of behavior through which conscious energy flows, if there is an essential reciprocity between personhood and consciousness, so that where one finds a unique and distinctive consciousness, there one also must discover a separate person, different from every other, then can we say that Jesus had two consciousnesses operating at different levels, divine and human? Would we not then in effect be saying that he had two personhoods, one divine and one human? Admittedly, we are dealing with the deepest mystery every time we broach the issue of the incarnation. But even a mystery cannot sustain the simultaneous affirmative predication of contraries. That would be a logical chimera, not a mystery. The key question is: is it possible for us to affirm the integration of two distinct consciousnesses into one functional personhood? Does it not pose a real problem for the believer today to affirm that Jesus' human consciousness or awareness allowed him, as a person, to grow, to expand, to become more certain of himself, while his divine consciousness already assured him that he had it made, that no further growth, expansion, of certitude was possible since he is indeed the Son of God? Certainly, apart from logic, it exceeds the powers of our imagination to try to envision a single person with two distinct consciousnesses: one which is perfect and absolute, encompassing selfhood, God and all creation, and the other which is severely limited and initially in an infantile state, but which eventually grows and develops just like our own.

To be sure, the mystery we grapple with here is not merely the mystery of the incarnation, a mystery perhaps more perplexing than that of the Trinity itself, but also the psychological mystery of just what constitutes personhood, and how precisely it is related to consciousness. Perhaps the best we can do is simply let the issue remain where it is: two unsolvable mysteries, one theological and the other psychological. But it is my suspicion that if modern psychology has complicated the question of the incarnation by heaping mystery upon mystery, modern physics might possibly offer an avenue to explore to see if the mystery of the incarnation might be able to sit a little more easily with a modern audience. Before we do this, however, we have to take into account what our tradition has said about the consciousness and knowledge of Jesus.

The Roman Catholic Church has issued a number of statements referring to the knowledge and consciousness of Jesus. None of these, however, seems to have been promulgated with the full doctrinal authority of the magisterium. There are no conciliar definitions or infallible papal decrees regarding this issue. All seem reformable, like the teaching of Pope Pius XII in his encyclical *Humani generis,* which we have already considered. The Bull *Quanta Cura* of Pope Pius IX, issued in 1864, condemns as errors a number of propositions which we today, after the Second Vatican Council would consider true. For instance, it was, at the time of Pius IX, considered erroneous that people can save their souls in any religious group or ecclesial community apart from Roman Catholicism, or that it would not be good to have Roman Catholicism as a state religion. In his encyclical letter *Mystici corporis* (On the Mystical Body) Pope Pius XII did teach that Jesus Christ had the beatific vision from the time of his conception, and so was able to pursue his mission of love from the very first moment of his existence as a human being. Pope Gregory the Great, in a letter he sent to Bishop Eulogius, scored the idea that Jesus might not have known the exact time of the final consummation of the world. He states that the Scripture passages which reflect this ignorance must be referred to the Mystical Christ, not to the Incarnate Word. They express, therefore, the ignorance of the Church, and not of Christ. The most formidable challenge, however, comes from the Constitution of Pope Vigilius, levelled in the sixth century against the Nestorians, which denies that Jesus did not know the future or the day of the last judgment and that he could know only as much as was revealed to him by the divinity which resided in him as in another being. It is true that theologians today generally do not regard this Constitution as a definition of faith. But even if it were, the heart of the problem that arose from the Nestorian view of Jesus lay in the fact that the divinity resided in him as in an alien being: that the divinity made itself present in Jesus as in a temple. This would have been the object of any definition, not necessarily what flowed from it, namely the ignorance, therefore, displayed by Jesus of any divine event that God, dwelling in him, did not directly reveal to him. The pope was not about to condemn a Gospel statement.

When, on the other hand, we come to consider the personhood of Jesus, we are confronted with dogmatic statements. The councils have defined that there is only one person in Jesus, and that is a divine person, that of the Logos, the Word, the Son of God. Until modern psychological considerations of personhood arrived on the scene there was not much difficulty in holding this. A simple test was devised. The person is what corresponds to the question: who? Who was born of the Virgin? Who died on the cross? The Logos. Even today it is possible for theologians to prescind from the deeper questions regarding the relationship between personality and consciousness, and say: yes,

Jesus did have a human personality in the psychological sense; that is, there were certain characteristics, certain ways of speaking and behaving that were distinctively his, and that would have shown up in any psychological testing anyone might have employed to mark him as a well-balanced, wonderful personality. But his *personhood,* his *person* is that of the Second Person of the Trinity. Any problems we have are due to our inability to comprehend the mystery of the incarnation.

In the previous chapter we considered how time contracts relative to earth aboard a spaceship that is traveling at a speed approaching that of light. We considered the case of a planet that is situated closer to an event in outer space than earth, and how even contradictory statements can be considered simultaneously true about that event from the perspective of earth, on one hand, and that of the planet, on the other. God does not exist in any dimensional system, but, as God, is above them all. We pointed out, however, that the creatures who are with him, the angels and the elect, are in eternity with him and so may constitute what we can call God's system. Here there is no time nor place as we know it. The only thing we can know about it really is that one of its parameters is, not unending time, but eternity, a continuous now. We know how difficult it is to let loose of the trappings of time when we try to project what that system might be like. But we can think of a never ceasing now which envelops and wraps up for us all the separate moments that seem in a kind of endless

fashion to be payed out for us on earth. Here the
perpetual present encompasses past, present and
future. Although there may be process in that
system, there is no gain or loss and so no way of
measuring time. Everything there is just the way it
is. There is no becoming, only what actually *is*.
That is why this system is so different from ours
where we continuously experience becoming, and
suffer the loss continuously of the last second and
look forward constantly to the gain of the next.
Outside of our intellect, in our system we really
never can get to what really *is*. Only through myth
and symbol can we reach the perfect, the absolute,
the unchanging.

The mystery of the incarnation must always remain just that. But perhaps some light can be shed
upon the complication of the mystery that emanates from the psychological know-how of the man
on the street today through the application of some
techniques of systems-analysis and the general principle of relativity.

When we ask, "Who is Jesus really?" we must
say that he is the Logos, the Son of God, Second
Person of the Trinity, and as such he existed eternally independent of any system. His personhood is
simply to be Logos. But as we know him on earth,
as we know him in our system, could he be the
human being who is destined at his resurrection to
be revealed as the Logos? Could it be that in our
system in his pre-resurrection existence he had not
yet become the Logos for us; the eternal event had
not yet reached us, just as news of the heavenly

cataclysm involving star X 645 would not become an event for us until 5000 years after it was confirmed on planet M 893 and 10,000 years after it actually took place?

Is it possible that in the eternity system, where everything is complete and absolute, where the whole truth about everything lies fully uncovered and displayed before every consciousness in the system, that we can affirm that this Logos was generated by his heavenly Father from all eternity, and that from the first moment of his conception we must affirm him to be identified with the human being we know as Jesus of Nazareth, while in the space-time system this person Jesus is generated and comes to the full consciousness of his position as Logos only at the time of the resurrection? It would be then that men, too, could discover who he really is and come to a full understanding and appreciation of him and his mission. Would he have been then in two different systems at the same time?

As man, no; he would be only in space-time up until the time of his resurrection and have only the consciousness of that system; as God he is above as well as the ground of all systems (simultaneously transcendent and immanent) and apprehended in each according to the modality of the system itself. Would he have to have two consciousnesses then and be open to the possibility of being misunderstood as being really two persons? By no means — no more than any being standing on the event horizon between two systems would have to have two consciousnesses. There are two systems, but not two consciousnesses. The conscious part, as it were, of the Logos which juts into our system from the event horizon assumes the parameters of the system itself; it is limited and can grow, as confirmed by our own consciousness of the system. But in this particular case, the part of it, as it were, on the other side of the event horizon is unlimited and outside of any system. Like the tip of the iceberg his consciousness is only partially revealed and used in our system, and the mode of its appearance and operation is perfectly attuned to the system. But in accordance with the rules of systems analysis (as well as those of theology) there is no admixture or mingling of the two systems: one consciousness, but two distinct systems. To use the analogy employed in the last chapter (poor as it is in illustrating this deep mystery of faith) a person situated in outer space (where he can observe the events taking place on X 645, M 893 and earth), if he could be conscious of what people are thinking and doing on earth, and would really want to be part of their experience and life, in order to be appreciated at all would have to affirm that he, too, like others, is taken with the beauty of X 645, even though he knows in the other system that is is really no longer extant. If he were to state this fact from his awareness of the other system, he would be laughed to scorn, or maybe put into an insane asylum (or in Jesus' time considered possessed by a devil). What people see and observe, they know exists. Even an incarnate God has to respect the given situation of the system in which he finds himself if he does not appear as God in that system.

If one should say that to affirm simultaneously the fact that the eternal Logos is indeed identified with Jesus of Nazareth from the first moment of his earthly existence, and that on earth Jesus became fully conscious of his identity as Logos at the time of his resurrection involves a contradiction, and therefore cannot be so — he simply would not have understood what we are trying to say. Such a person would not have let loose of time when dealing with the other system and would have projected this parameter of our system into it. Or, what is worse, such a person may have introjected an eternal reality as eternal into our system. What is eternal can exist in our system only as revelation, not as reality, as thought, not as being. If one tries to bring God as he is in himself into our system, he assays the impossible; he tries to put him where he cannot exist formally. Infinity cannot be squeezed into a finite dimensional system. It can inhabit that system only in an intentional way, principally through faith.

This is not to say that the impact of divinity cannot be felt in our system; the effects of God's operation are marvelously perceived in our system; though he may not be present in a perceptible substantial way, he is with us in his works of power and love. As we said before, God cannot appear in any positive way in our consciousness. As Karl Rahner intimates, when God decided to appear in our system, he had very little choice. He had to appear as

man. Man is a natural stand-in for God. Man, as
Rahner says, is the cipher for God, the abbrevi-
ation of God, the code-word for God in our system. The fact that man is the image of God was indeed God's revelation to man from the beginning,
but man always tries to reject this truth: he cannot
believe that he really is an image of God, and is
called to reflect him in his own striving after
goodness and perfection. This revelation had to be
and was in no common measure restated in Christ.
Even as man he was indeed the Son of God, but this
tremendous truth was only gradually to be discovered even by himself in our system, and to be
fully revealed only in the resurrection.

The heart of the mystery of the incarnation is
hidden in the question of the consciousness of
Jesus. How can the consciousness of a single person pervade two different systems with such radically different appreciations? Can we say that Jesus
is fully conscious of just who he is only in God's
world, as God; here his consciousness is unlimited?
But he could not bring that infinite consciousness
with him into our system. It simply cannot support
the infinite in any positive way. It is space-time, a
very limited system. Only after the resurrection
could he appreciate as a human being in another
system who he really is; only then could his human
consciousness, his perspective on our world, accept
him as he is in himself, as his divine consciousness,
his perspective into infinity always affirmed him to
be — not as if there were two consciousnesses,
which would imply a divided self, but two out-

reachings of the same awareness, one groping experientially in this world, and the other possessing all in another — one consciousness interfaced between two systems.

Jesus is called the Logos, the Word, the Concept of God. Logos is a product of consciousness. From all eternity the divine Logos was generated by his Father in the intellect of the Godhead. He is the perfect reflection of his Father, the perfect imaging of God in God, of exactly the same substance as the Father. He is the double of the Father, his replica, the one who shares exactly the same nature with the Father. This generation of the Son in the consciousness of God was, as we have said, from all eternity. But he is also generated as Logos in our system; he becomes Logos in his own and other human beings' consciousness at the time of his resurrection, when the full revelation is made in our system of just who he is, that he is indeed the double image of the Father. Before that could we say that in our system he had only a subconscious awareness of his real identity?

Did Jesus, if he was not fully conscious of just who he was in our system during his lifetime, experience in some way his identity? Although experience originates from consciousness and is based upon consciousness, it is not exactly coterminous with consciousness. Experience is easily related to our positive consciousness. What we are aware of we experience. But it is also possible for us to have an experience of negative consciousness, and so experience is a much wider concept than consciousness. In sleep one's consciousness is certainly greatly reduced. In sleep the terminator of one's consciousness is brought very close to the center of one's being. Yet to sleep is to have an authentic human experience, albeit a negative one in respect to consciousness. To be in a deep coma is also to have a real human experience, yet here one is almost totally deprived of consciousness as we know it.

It is not possible simultaneously to have experience in two different systems. As we said before, one must be substantially in one or the other. Although one can be conscious of more than one system, it does not seem possible that he can experience two simultaneously. God does not have experience properly so called; we experience. With God, Jesus' consciousness is not an experiential one; he experiences and consequently is located only in our system, only in space-time, not in the bosom of his Father in union with the Spirit.

But in our system did Jesus during his lifetime experience himself as God? I would say most likely he did, but only from the dark side of his consciousness, only from beyond the terminator, only in his subconscious mind. There are inklings of his appreciation of this fact in the synoptic Gospels. But of course, after his resurrection, he becomes fully conscious of his identity as God. And could we say that when he comes to the full awareness of just who he is even in our system, when he responds to the Father's call to the resurrected life, that then he is generated as Logos even in our system?

Yes, it is a mystery how the same person could have such radically different consciousnesses in two totally different systems, how one and the same person could even exist simultaneously in two diverse systems in such fundamentally different ways. For creatures certainly this is not possible. But we are dealing with a divine person. As was said before, one who is divine can in his infinity encompass contrary realities simultaneously. If it is possible for God in himself to be both immutable and in process at the same time, we should be able to envision him as existing in himself and in our dimensional system at the same time. Perhaps we cannot understand it fully, but we do believe it.

Karl Rahner and other theologians see consciousness as related to being itself in conscious beings. Consciousness is reflected existence. Could we not say that if theologians have seen it possible that in Christ there is one single existent, there has then to be in Christ one single consciousness?

The Church's magisterium largely pursues a Christology from above. The revelation that the Church has received gives it a window on the eternity system. Consequently its dogmas and pronouncements have the ring of absolute finality about them. Only in the eternity system can things be absolutely what they are. Researchers and theologians, on the other hand, tend to pursue today a Christology from below. That is why their findings have to be provisional and tentative. They must deal with data that are ambiguous and incomplete, and rely on historical methodology. So often the best they can do is simply to pose certain questions and hope that the future will be able to supply answers.

If one were to say, however, that from the time of Pope Vigilius down to the present the Church has always taught that the divine Word was united to Jesus from the first moment of his conception in the womb of the Virgin, how could a response be made by one who would hold that Jesus was generated as the Word of God at the time of his resurrection? One who would ask such a question or pose such a difficulty would have missed the whole point in applying the principle of relativity to the issue. From the perspective of the eternity system which sees things as they really are, totally uncovered and in their final state, one could make this absolute pronouncement. But from the perspective of our system, though Jesus had this identity from the beginning, it was covered over, concealed and hidden like the identity of all human beings in the beginning. We have to struggle through our lifetime to discover something about ourselves, who we are and who we would like to be, and it will not be revealed to us either who we really are with absolute definition and finality until we enter the other system. Yet Jesus was a man just like us. He experienced what we experience in the space-time continuum. He grew into his identity during his lifetime, but was in full possession of it only after entering the other system through his death. Jesus' consciousness in our system had to be like ours, did it not? Otherwise how could we say that he is indeed fully human? Final state, full uncovering of the truth, end of the process, the absolute: these can exist only in God's system; there there is no becoming, no process implying growth, gain or loss; becoming and this kind of process are the tools of our trade; they are the characteristics of our system of space-time.

We have very tentatively, but hopefully also, applied both traditional theological data and scientific theoretical principles to the question of Christ's personhood and consciousness. Two seemingly disparate fields have been cross-fertilized to see what might emerge. It is to be hoped that it will be a better understanding of the universe in which we live, and a deepening of the faith to which we firmly adhere.

BIBLIOGRAPHY

Baltazar, E. *Teilhard and the Supernatural.* Baltimore, Maryland: Helicon, 1966.

Baum, G. *Man Becoming.* New York: Herder & Herder, 1970.

Bonhöffer, D. *Letters and Papers from Prison.* New York: Macmillan, 1962.

Boros, L. *The Mystery of Death.* New York: Herder & Herder, 1965.

Cobb, J. *A Christian Natural Theology: Based on the Thought of Alfred North Whitehead.* Philadelphia: Westminster Press, 1965.

————. *The Structure of Christian Existence.* Philadelphia: Westminster Press, 1967.

————. *God and the World.* Philadelphia: Westminster Press, 1969.

Congregation for the Doctrine of the Faith. *Letter on Certain Questions Concerning Eschatology.* May 17, 1979. Washington, D.C.: *Origins,* 9, 131, August 2, 1979.

Cox, H. *The Secular City.* New York: Macmillan, 1965.

Däniken, E. von. *Gods from Outer Space: Return to the Stars or Evidence For the Impossible.* New York: Putnam, 1971.

————. *Chariots of the Gods? Unsolved Mysteries of the Past.* New York: Putnam, 1969.

Davies, P. C. *The Physics of Time Asymmetry.* Berkeley, California: University of California Press, 1974.

Dingle, H. *The Special Theory of Relativity.* London: Methuen and Company, 1950.

Feinberg, G. *What is the World Made of? Atoms, Leptons, Quarks, and Other Tantalizing Particles.* New York: Doubleday, 1977.

Fortman, E. *Everlasting Life After Death*. New York: Alba House, 1976.

Gilkey, L. *Catholicism Confronts Modernity: A Protestant View*. New York: Seabury, 1975.

———. *Naming the Whirlwind. The Renewal of God-Language*. Indianapolis: Bobbs-Merrill, 1969.

———. *Reaping the Whirlwind. A Christian Interpretation of History*. New York: Seabury, 1976.

Godin, A. *Death and Presence: The Psychology of Death in the After Life*. Brussels, Belgium: Lumen Vitae Press, 1972.

Gutwenger, E. *Bewusstsein und Wissen Christi: eine dogmatische Studie*. Innsbruck: Rauch, 1960.

Hartshorne, C. *A Natural Theology for our Time*. LaSalle, Illinois: Open Court, 1967.

Heidegger, M. *Being and Time*. New York: Harper, 1962.

———. *Existence and Being*. Chicago: H. Regnery Company, 1949.

Heisenberg, W. *Physics and Beyond*. New York: Harper and Row, 1971.

Hellwig, M. *What Are They Saying about Death and Christian Hope?* New York: Paulist Press, 1978.

Hick, J. *Death and Eternal Life*. New York: Harper & Row, 1976.

Houston, W. *Principles of Quantum Mechanics*. New York: McGraw-Hill, 1951.

James, W. *The Varieties of Religious Experience*. New York: Mentor, 1958.

Jammarrone, L. *L'unità psicologica in Christo*. Roma: Editrice "Miscellanea Francescana," 1962.

Jammer, M. *The Philosophy of Quantum Mechanics*. New York: Wiley and Sons, 1974.

Kelly, H. *The Devil, Demonology and Witchcraft*. New York: Doubleday, 1968.

Kübler-Ross, E. *Death: The Final Stage of Growth*. Englewood Cliffs, N.J., 1975.

———. *On Death and Dying*. New York: Macmillan, 1969.

Lonergan, B. *De constitutione Christi ontologica et psychologica supplementum.* Romae: Universitas Gregoriana, 1956.

May, R. *Love and Will.* New York: Norton, 1969.

———. *Power and Innocence.* New York: Norton, 1972.

McShane, P. *Randomness, Statistics and Emergence.* Notre Dame, Indiana: University of Notre Dame Press, 1970.

Metz, J. *Theology of the World.* New York: Herder & Herder, 1969.

Molari, C. *De Christi ratione essendi et operandi.* Romae: Officium Libri Catholici, 1957.

Moltmann, J. *The Theology of Hope: On the Grounded Implications of a Christian Eschatology.* New York: Harper & Row, 1967.

Moody, R. *Life After Life.* Atlanta, Georgia: Mockingbird Books, 1975.

Nowell, R. *What a Modern Catholic Believes about Death.* Chicago: Thomas More Press, 1972.

Ogden, S. *The Reality of God and Other Essays.* New York: Harper & Row, 1966.

Pagels, H. *The Cosmic Code: Quantum Physics as the Language of Nature.* New York: Simon and Schuster, 1982.

Papin, J., Ed. *The Eschaton: A Community of Love.* Villanova, Pennsylvania: Villanova University Press, 1971.

Parente, P. *L' Io di Christo.* Brescia, Morcelliana, 1955.

Pieper, J. *Death and Immortality.* New York: Herder & Herder, 1969.

Pittenger, W. N. *Process-Thought in Christian Faith.* New York: Macmillan, 1968.

———. *'The Last Things' in a Process Perspective.* London: Epworth Press, 1970.

Pius XII, Pope. *Humani generis: Encyclical Letter Concerning Some False Opinions which Threaten to Undermine the Foundations of Catholic Doctrine.* Washington, D.C.: National Catholic Welfare Conference, 1950.

Reitdijk, C. *On Waves, Particles and Hidden Variables.* Assen, Holland: Van Gorcum, 1971.

Bibliography

Rondet, H. *Original Sin: The Patristic and Theological Background*. New York: Alba House, 1972.

Satan. New York: Sheed and Ward, 1952.

Schillebeeckx, E. *God, The Future of Man*. New York: Sheed & Ward, 1968.

——. *The Problem of Eschatology*. New York: Paulist Press, 1969.

——. *Jesus: An Experiment in Christology*. New York: Seabury, 1979.

——. *Christ: The Experience of Jesus as Lord*. New York: Seabury, 1980.

Schoonenberg, P. *God's World in the Making*. Pittsburgh, Pennsylvania: Duquesne University Press, 1964.

Schwarz, H. *Our Cosmic Journey*. Minneapolis, Minnesota: Augsburg, 1977.

Shea, J. *What a Modern Catholic Believes about Heaven and Hell*. Chicago: The Thomas More Press, 1972.

Shepherd, W. *Man's Condition: God and the World Process*. New York: Herder & Herder, 1968.

Simpson, M. *The Theology of Death and Eternal Life*. Notre Dame, Indiana: Fides, 1971.

Slater, J. *Quantum Theory of Matter*. New York: McGraw-Hill, 1951.

Stevenson, K., and Haberman, G. *Verdict on the Shroud*. Ann Arbor, Michigan: Servant Books, 1981.

Teilhard de Chardin, P. *The Phenomenon of Man*. New York: Harper and Row, 1965.

——. *The Divine Milieu*. New York: Harper and Row, 1965.

——. *The Future of Man*. New York: Harper and Row, 1965.

Temple, G. *The General Principles of Quantum Theory*. London: Methuen and Company, 1951.

Troisfontaines, R. *I Do Not Die*. New York: Desclée, 1963.

Vahanian, G. *Wait Without Idols*. New York: George Braziller, 1964.

Van Buren, P. *Theological Explorations*. New York: Macmillan, 1968.

Whelan, J., Ed. *The God Experience: Essays in Hope*. New York: Newman, 1971.

Whitehead, A. N. *Process and Reality: An Essay in Cosmology*. New York: Macmillan, 1929.

Xiberta y Roqeta, B. *El yo de Jesu Christo: un conflicto entre dos Christologias*. Barcelona: Editorial Herder, 1954.